"An Aspirant's Guide to Practicing The Egyptian Mysteries"

The Everyday Practice of the Egyptian Mysteries (Shetaut Neter) From an Initiates Perspective

Discernment and Discriminative Knowledge of
What is Real and What is Not Real.

Lawrence R. Mathews J.D., B.B.A.
(Anpu Waset)

"An Aspirant's Guide To Practicing The Egyptian Mysteries"

11120 West Van Buren Suite #2129
Avondale, AZ 85323
480-495-3309
lrmathews60@yahoo.com
www.inspirationalphilosophy.com

Published by LAWRENCE R. MATHEWS

Copyright ©2011

LAWRENCE R. MATHEWS
All rights reserved. No part of this book may be used or reproduced in any manner whatsoever without the written permission (address above) of the author.

Book Cover Design by Lawrence R. Mathews
Book Cover Photos by Lawrence R. Mathews
Insert Graphics courtesy of Dr. Muata Ashby

The author is available for lectures and may be reached at the address above.

ISBN: 0-9786346-3-2

"An Aspirant's Guide To Practicing The Egyptian Mysteries"

NEBERDJER

The All Encompassing Divinity

"Do Not Allow What You Think or How You Think to LIMIT What You Think or How You Think!"

By: Anpu Waset

"An Aspirant's Guide To Practicing The Egyptian Mysteries"

Table of Contents

Dedication... 7

Special Dedication.. 8

Author's Forward... 9

Background.. 12

Introduction... 15

The Qualities of An Authentic Aspirant............................... 19

SECTION ONE
I Found It! This Is It!

Chapter 1
I Found It! This Is It! 35

Chapter 2
Congratulate Yourself & Trust the Process......................... 43

Chapter 3
General Considerations of the Impact of Your Study
of the Teachings on Members of Your Family.................... 49

Chapter 4
What Does It Mean to Practice Ancient
"Mystical" Spirituality?.. 59

Chapter 5
What is Shetaut Neter and its Purpose?.............................. 63

SECTION TWO
Common Obstacles while Engaged in the
Daily Practice of Shetaut Neter

Chapter 6
Belief in Gender.. 67

Chapter 7
Something to Consider, Ideas Shape Reality............................. 73

Chapter 8
The Relationship between the Spiritual
Preceptor & the World.. 81

Chapter 9
What You See, Is What You Get!... 87

Chapter 10
Recognizing "Real" Hellish Conditions...................................... 93

Chapter 11
Lost In the World... 99

Chapter 12
And the World Comes Tumbling Down!....................................105

Chapter 13
Holding Onto the World of Mental Agitation........................... 111

Chapter 14
The Holy War Within... 117

SECTION THREE
Sheti Disciplines in Everyday Practice

Chapter 15
Righteousness in Action (Maat)... 137

Chapter 16
Wisdom in Practice (Rekh)...147

Chapter 17
Devotion in Practice (Ushet)... 153

Chapter 18
Meditation in Practice (Uaa)...165

Chapter 19
The Three Fold Sheti Practice..169

Chapter 20
Conclusion.. 173

About the Author.. 182

"An Aspirant's Guide To Practicing The Egyptian Mysteries"

DEDICATION

    This book is dedicated to the Aspirants of the Ancient African Egyptian Philosophy and Religion known as "Shetaut Neter." This philosophy and religion was known as the "Egyptian Mysteries" for those outside of its practice. What is presented is a guide from an Initiates point of view of what practicing the teachings in day to day life looks like. Although the teachings are relatively simple to understand intellectually, their application in everyday life is anything but easy. How do you know if you're practicing the teachings correctly? What will be encountered as the full integration of the teachings is merged into your daily life? What can be done today that will allow your spiritual practice to minimize the occurrence of ups and downs? These questions and more are answered in this work. This book is for those who would like an additional aid/guide to assist them in their pursuit/achievement of Nehast in this lifetime. It is written and should be used as a supplement to the book "Initiation into Egyptian Yoga and Neterianism" by Dr. Muata Ashby as it provides the practical application of those teachings to everyday life.

"An Aspirant's Guide To Practicing The Egyptian Mysteries"

Special Dedication

You may already be aware that highest achievement in life, Nehast/Enlightenment, is most easily obtained when an authentic teaching is presented by an authentic teacher to an authentic aspirant. For those who study the ancient path of Shetaut Neter (Hidden Mysteries) you are aware that we have in our midst two authentic teachers in Sebai Maa (Dr. Muata Ashby) and Seba Dja (Dr. Karen Clark Ashby).

On behalf of the entire Neterian community we would like you both to know that your "selfless service" in the resurrection and dissemination of this ancient tradition is truly appreciated.

Sebai Maa **Seba Dja**

Dua M Htp!

"An Aspirant's Guide To Practicing The Egyptian Mysteries"

Author's Forward

The Qualities of An Authentic Aspirant

Nehast is the term used to describe the highest form of awareness of 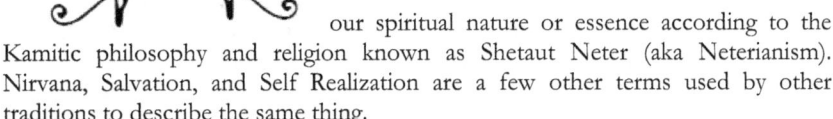 our spiritual nature or essence according to the Kamitic philosophy and religion known as Shetaut Neter (aka Neterianism). Nirvana, Salvation, and Self Realization are a few other terms used by other traditions to describe the same thing.

To achieve this "awareness a.k.a. awakened state," the Neterian tradition of Ancient Kamit enjoins that three things are needed:

1. An authentic teaching/religion;
2. An authentic teacher; and
3. An authentic aspirant/student.

1. An Authentic Teaching/Religion

In brief an authentic teaching/religion, number one above, is one that is composed of a threefold set of practices. **Myth, ritual**, and a **mystical practice** are the foundation of an authentic teaching and/or religion. Any teaching or religion that does not contain all three is not an authentic teaching. Any teaching which has all three components but discounts, minimizes, or discards altogether one or more of these three is also not authentic.

2. An Authentic Teacher

The book, "Glorious Light Meditation," by Dr. Muata Ashby, on page 41, discusses the qualities of an authentic teacher which is number two above. According to him, such a person is known as a "Spiritual Preceptor" and can be described as follows.

"**A Spiritual Preceptor is not only a person who has attained a high level of internal self-discovery and purity, but also a person who is well versed in the scriptural writings and has knowledge of parables and myths** along with their mystical implications. He or she also knows the practices which lead a person to spiritual evolution (Yoga disciplines)."

A Spiritual Preceptor (authentic teacher) is further described in the book, "Initiation Into Egyptian Yoga and Neterian Spirituality also by Dr. Ashby. On page 67 he states the following about a Spiritual Preceptor.

"An authentic Spiritual Preceptor is not only someone who is advanced on the spiritual path or even just someone who has reached the fully enlightened state. A Guru, in the Upanishadic (teachings of the Indian Upanishads) sense of the word, is someone who is spiritually enlightened and who also is well versed in the scriptural teachings and methods of training aspirants according to their level of understanding. Therefore, a counselor of Yoga must first achieve a high degree of understanding and personal-spiritual emancipation since the subtleties of the mind must be well understood. The teacher must be able to be a refuge for all people, have an extensive knowledge of the teachings pertaining to his/her level of attainment, and enthusiastically pursue all forms of Yoga.

An authentic teacher of yoga philosophy is someone who is advanced on the path of self-control, one who is indifferent to either positive or negative situations which arise, one who is not affected by praise or censure and is not desirous of any object in the phenomenal world. He or she has discovered inner fulfillment and is a well spring of joy to all whom they come into contact with. They are not interested in developing relationships with students based upon emotionality or other egoistic sensibilities and they are not interested in keeping disciples as servants for their own amusement or in keeping company to inflate their own egos because they have transcended all of these human frailties. They are fulfilled through their realization of their own divinity and help others out of compassion and universal love which flows through them directly from the divine source."

3. An Authentic Aspirant

This book deals specifically with the third aspect above and details the qualities of an authentic aspirant. Although a major treatise could be written on the first two, the concentration and focus of this work are on what qualities an aspirant can develop which will assist you to "best" be able to benefit from *authentic teachings provided by an authentic teacher.* Simply put, the highest teachings of authentic spirituality can be given by the highest person qualified to teach them. However,

"An Aspirant's Guide To Practicing The Egyptian Mysteries"

these teachings mean nothing if given to a person who lacks the qualities to practice them as provided.

What are those qualities? Essentially there are four of them.

1. Desire for the teachings;
2. Belief that the teachings will work for you;
3. Spiritual vigilance; and
4. Good association.

I will discuss these in detail shortly. Be aware that as soon as you begin to implement the "complete" practices of Shetaut Neter into your daily life, you are deemed to be an authentic aspirant. The qualities that will now be discussed when cultivated aid in the purification process as you learn how to master yourself. For clarity though I want you to be aware that I am a Priest of the Temple of Aset. My title is Unut. The information provided in this book is based upon the experiences that I and other aspirants have had while being practitioners of the teachings of Shetaut Neter. Shetaut Neter means *"hidden mysteries or mysteries of the Divine."* It is my desire that you through your reading of these words will better know what to expect as you begin your practice of authentic spirituality. The specific qualities of an authentic aspirant are detailed now as well as typical experiences that you can expect to have as a practitioner of an authentic religious system. Both will help you better deal with your daily practical life situations as you integrate authentic spiritual practices into it.

If you are new to the teachings of Shetaut Neter this book is for you. If you have practiced some other form of spirituality that contains the three components of *myth, ritual, and mysticism,* this book is for you also. There is a similar basis to all authentic spiritual systems so that once one practice is well known, others can be easily understood.

In short, this book is for all people who would like to do two things:

1. Identify the qualities of an authentic aspirant; and
2. Discover what to expect in your day to day life as you practice the teachings of authentic spirituality.

"An Aspirant's Guide To Practicing The Egyptian Mysteries"

Background

This book has been written for the person presently seeking the answer to the age old question Who Am I? Although the who am I question has been asked by many generations of people over many years, since the closing of the The Temple of Aset, the ancient Kamitic methodology used for discovering its answer has been forgotten. When Emperor Constantine of Rome decreed in approximately 313 A.D., that the new world religion would be Christianity, thousands of years of highly advanced African philosophy and religion were cast aside. Prior to this decree, the ancient Egyptian methods used to answer the higher questions in life were done thru the use of *myth, ritual and mysticism*. Since those fateful times, mysticism has not been used as a means towards this end.

Myth → Ritual → Mysticism

The underlying basis for using *myth, ritual and mysticism*, was the belief that the underlying essence at the core of Creation and everything in it is Divine Essence/Consciousness or God. Therefore from the perspective of ancient cultures, every person has the ability to discover this Divine Essence/Consciousness or God by simply going within him or herself. Mysticism is the process that allows a person to go within and discover this. The only thing needed for this method to work as mentioned earlier is an *authentic teaching, an authentic teacher*, and you as the student must be an *authentic aspirant*.

If you are reading this book you have either chosen this ancient method of answering the higher questions of life or are strongly considering it. This method has been expressed thru many cultures of the ancient world but was founded and expressed in its highest form through the Ancient African land of Kamit/Egypt. Their ancient belief systems make it clear that you cannot have a relationship with who/what you consider to be God if you are not "identifying" with the Godly aspect of your nature. In this belief system this identification can only occur thru the mystical process.

This is one of the biggest differences between religion and philosophy as practiced in ancient times and how it has been practiced since 313 A.D. Since Constantine's decree, people stopped believing that they had a Divine or Godly aspect to their nature. Since that time, this Divine nature was thought to exist with only Jesus in Christianity and Prophet Muhammad in Islam.

"An Aspirant's Guide To Practicing The Egyptian Mysteries"

You may have now begun the "practice" of incorporating *myth, ritual,* and *mysticism* into your daily life. For purposes of this book, practice means living your life in such a way that you allow yourself to "experience" the higher transcendental aspect of your nature. Practice in this context also means that you have begun to change your lifestyle so that this realization can occur.

The individual practice discussed in this book is based upon the ancient Kamitic Religion and Philosophy of Shetaut Neter. You may also be a student of other ancient African religious and philosophical systems. Others may be students of the Ancient Eastern traditions of Buddhism, Hinduism, Confucianism and Taoism.

Whatever your discipline, this book will assist you as you begin to live your life in accordance with ancient philosophical and religious precepts. This lifestyle change will make a positive change in your personality. However, change even for the good can be rocky until the change becomes permanent. Knowing what to expect while on this new lifestyle is the major aim of this book.

One thing that you may not be aware of as you begin living your life spiritually thru the ancient practices composed of *myth, ritual and mysticism* is the affect it will have on those people in your inner circle. Additionally it is difficult to know at the beginning how your new practice will change the way interactions with other people will be either. Your new practice will be challenging for you personally as you will learn about the negative aspects of your personality and then go about purifying them. However, the biggest challenge which you should expect to get is the reaction you will receive from your family and friends when introducing your new spiritual practice to them.

In many ways dealing with these reactions will be just as difficult and sometimes more difficult as dealing with the discovery of your own personal issues. This is because people tend to want acceptance from those people that they are the closest to. When you find that your new practice will not be accepted by the people you love most in the world, it is difficult not to be disheartened. If you don't expect this at the beginning of your practice, this may create a mental challenge that can take years to overcome. The reality is that very few family members or close friends will gravitate towards the teachings like you have. This is not a bad or good thing. It's just the way it is. The sooner this is realized, the sooner you will eliminate a cause of frustration on your spiritual journey. However their failure to adopt your lifestyle should not be looked at with discouragement. Your impact on your family members and close friends will be great. As they see you discipline yourself and handle life's challenges in a higher way, their conscious will be moved in a higher way as well.

In this work you will find information about what to expect in your daily everyday world as ancient spiritual practices are integrated into your life. Armed with this knowledge, your movement to discover the answer to the question "Who Am I?" will occur in the quickest way possible.

"An Aspirant's Guide To Practicing The Egyptian Mysteries"

Introduction

This book has been written specifically to be a supplement to the book written by Dr. Muata Ashby (Sebai Maa) called "Initiation into Egyptian Yoga and Neterian Spirituality." The "Initiation" book is a practitioner's guide to implementing Kemetic Spiritual Disciplines into your daily life. It provides the aspirant with instruction on how to take the first steps on the Ancient Egyptian path to Self-Mastery, Immortality and Enlightenment. It provides great details about spiritual emancipation and the specific practices done by the Ancient Sages and Saints of Ancient Kamit to achieve this state. Most importantly, it shows the aspirant how those same practices can be applied today to also lead to this state.

The "Initiation" book provides specific practices done in Ancient Kamit. But Ancient Kamit was a much different place than the present 21st century. In Ancient Kamit, there was not a plethora of different religious practices. There was only one, Shetaut Neter. For those who wanted spiritual emancipation (salvation) there was only one place to go which was the Temple. Although not everyone who lived during that time was an enlightened sage, the entire community was aware of the 42 Precepts of Maat and lived their lives according to them. This work seeks to further bridge the differences between living a spiritual life in Ancient Kamit and today.

This book will also help beginning practitioners of other "mystical" religious and philosophical systems integrate these practices into their daily life. Mystical systems tend to have some things in common. One such thing is the lifestyle necessary to achieve spiritual liberation. They all have a lifestyle code of conduct to be employed by the new practitioner known as a purification process. Another thing common to mystical systems is that meditation is a significant part of the practice. Additionally, the point of view regarding the role played by the ego/personality of a person and how it leads a person to bondage to time and space is viewed similarly. Finally, these systems enjoin reflection on the wisdom teachings and a holistic outlook on life.

Now that you have decided to adopt Shetaut Neter or another ancient "mystical" system as your path to enlightenment, you will now begin to face certain challenges. One challenge will be the purification of the ego. Other challenges will occur as your spiritual practice matures.

This work provides you with what you can "expect" in your day to day life as the practices in the Initiation book are implemented. Some of the questions it will answer include but are not limited to the following.

-How will your family react to your new practice?
-How should you present the teachings of Shetaut Neter or your ancient mystical system to them?
-What about your friends and co-workers?
- What does spiritualizing every aspect of your life look like in every day life and will that change what you do on a typical day?
-How will you know if you are making progress on the spiritual path? Are you practicing the teachings correctly?

These questions and more are answered in this book.

If you are very excited about "discovering" a path to spiritual liberation do not be surprised. This discovery causes great joy and excitement in those ready to answer the higher questions in life. You may find yourself purchasing many books on the subject. You may read these books several times. Your conversation may become filled with your new found understanding of the teachings. In a certain way you may become fanatical. Fanatical for a good purpose as you are now attempting to live your life spiritually. But fanaticism for any reason can be harmful if awareness of its presence is lacking. In the world of spiritual practice if not handled properly, fanaticism can make your spiritual movement become disjointed.

For purposes of this book, fanaticism refers to actions done to practice the teachings without regard to how these practices will be received by those around you. It also means acting in such a way that you do most things according to the exact letter of the practice. Therefore, balance and reflection are lacking which prevents understanding of what the teaching is actually attempting to convey.

The new practitioner of Shetaut Neter is provided an outlook on implementing the practices from the Initiation book in an integrated way free from the common fanatical moments that many people have when they begin to implement spiritual practices into their daily life. The new and not so new practitioner will find common situations that typically develop for people who live their lives in a spiritual way. These situations involve family and friends. Most importantly, these situations involve you and your discovery of aspects of your personality that you were not previously aware of. Discovery of these aspects is necessary as they are a barrier to the full effect of the mystical process.

In conclusion this book provides a roadmap of sorts so that you know what to expect on this new path from those around you, how to deal with them and how to measure whether or not you're implementing the practice effectively.

"An Aspirant's Guide To Practicing The Egyptian Mysteries"

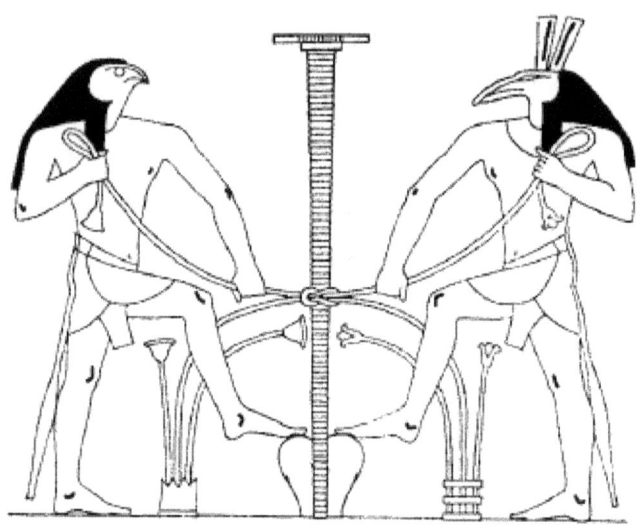

Figure 5: Above: Smai Heru-Set,

The Qualities of An Authentic Aspirant

The qualities of an authentic aspirant are qualities that are to be cultivated within your personality. Although they are not "what" you can expect as a practitioner of the teachings, their cultivation will help you integrate the practices of the teachings into your daily life. The "desire" to cultivate them and the everyday practice of them makes you an "authentic aspirant." Some people in the initial stages of their spiritual practice may immediately realize that they possess one or two of them. You may be one of these people. Others may find that they do not possess any of them. Rare are those who immediately exemplify all of them. If they did, they would not have had a reason to incarnate again into the world of time and space again☺. The decision to adopt and live your life with a spiritual lifestyle will have its greatest affect when you realize that cultivation of the attributes below will help you on your path to spiritual enlightenment.

Desire

The first quality found in authentic aspirants is "desire" for enlightenment. Without this type of desire would there be a reason to want to practice the teachings of Shetaut Neter or any other mystical tradition in the first place? Realistically, how can you become good at anything that you first don't want to do? Aren't we much better at doing things that we desire and enjoy rather than those that we don't? Although it may seem like a given, desire for the teachings and what the teachings help bring about is a very important quality to have.

Prior to your interest in books like this, you may have had and still may have a desire for many different things. Desire for a lot of money, certain types of relationships, fame, children, travel, to look a certain way, are all common desires of people today. Query? How many people do you know right now that desire spiritual awakening and realization? Right now in this moment is this "really" a desire of yours?

Query number two. Have you ever noticed what people with desires for things do? They think about their desires don't they? Many times they work to achieve them too right? And finally, they even talk about wanting them on a regular basis. I think then that it's safe to say that desire for things is good, because it provides a sort of energy that allows a person to move in a way that will helps them achieve things. The problem though is that few realize the difference between "worldly" desires and "spiritual" desires. Worldly desires are based on gaining something in the world. Objects and things which are perishable. Everything in creation is perishable because everything has a definite amount of time to live and be. Everything is born and everything will die. Many are they who base their pursuit of "eternal and unconditional" happiness in desires for things that are perishable. You can see that this practice is bound to lead to disappointment and pain.

Worldly desires although mistaken are really not the problem though. The mistaken belief that fulfillment of a "worldly" desire will produce unconditional happiness for a person is. If you think about this you know it to be true. How many times have you wanted something, a new car for example, and soon after getting it, your feelings about it changed? How long does it take before the novelty wears off? One, two, six months or a year? It doesn't last forever does it? This should be a warning flag letting us know that "worldly" desires of all kinds have the same outcome. None of them provide unconditional happiness. Unfortunately for many of us it's not. Instead since we don't know how to live life in any other way, we go from one desire to the next, working for it, thinking it will provide eternal happiness and joy, not becoming eternally fulfilled by it, and doing the process over and over again in an endless cycle.

An authentic aspirant is a person who has realized the "right" things to desire. The "right" things are those which upon receipt produce unconditional and eternal happiness. Therefore there really is only one thing worthy of desire and that in our tradition is called Nehast. The term Nehast means "to awaken" to higher consciousness.

Desires and their Relationship to the Thinking Process

In the book "Initiation Into Egyptian Yoga and Neterian Spirituality," by Dr. Muata Ashby, qualities of an authentic aspirant are discussed. The following ancient Egyptian precepts on initiatic education are mentioned on page 50:

1. "Control your thoughts,"
2. "Control your actions,"
3. "Have devotion of purpose,"
4. "Have faith in your master's ability to lead you along the path of truth,"
5. "Have faith in your own ability to accept the truth,"
6. "Have faith in your ability to act with wisdom,"
7. "Be free of resentment under the experience of persecution," (Bear insult)
8. "Be free from resentment under experience of wrong," (Bear injury)
9. "Learn how to distinguish between right and wrong,"

10. "Learn how to distinguish the real from the unreal."

I think it is safe to say that living your life based upon these precepts will qualify you as an authentic aspirant. But look at the first precept which says "control your thoughts." Have you ever attempted to control your thoughts? Were you able to do it? Assume in this moment that you would like to control your thoughts right now. Assume also that you have never done this before. How do you do it? Aren't thoughts things that come and go in and out of your mind without rhyme or reason? Do you know anyone that is actually able to control their thoughts? Notice that this is the "first" precept. Query. Does it stand to reason that the practice of the nine precepts that follow this one do so "after" one has first mastered this one?

What about controlling your actions? Have you ever attempted to control each and every action you engage in on a regular and sustained basis? Actions are probably easier to control than thoughts for some, but these are not that easy to control either. Especially those actions that occur in an "automatic" or "instant" way when triggered through life circumstances.

These first two precepts seem a bit surreal in that they are practices few people consider as possible for human beings to actually do. Today for many it is assumed that control over the thought process and control over certain actions is not possible. The remaining eight precepts seem to be practices that people can have an easier time exercising control over.

Although it might not seem like it, control of thoughts and actions is possible. The key to making this possible is to understand an aspect of the mind and how it operates. This is why "desire" to practice the teachings that lead to Nehast/Spiritual Realization is one of the important qualities that you will find in an authentic aspirant.

Desire plays a large role in the life of every person. Few understand how significant its role is. Many discount, minimize or dismiss it altogether. This is true of both a practitioner of the teachings of Shetaut Neter and of a worldly person also. The only difference between each is "what" they desire.

Did you know that the genesis of all thoughts and actions can be found at "desires" door? Every thought and consequently every action that you may have cannot come into being until you first have a desire for it. In fact, it is not possible to have a thought about something unless the desire was already present. This is because until desire for something is present, there is nothing to think about.

Consider the following example with certain kinds of food. You are aware that we as human beings need food for our daily sustenance. If I were to ask you the general question right now, "tell me about food," it is likely that nothing "specific" is coming into your mind. However, if I instead now say "tell me about your favorite food," something different happens doesn't it? Many thoughts are probably coming to your mind now. What's the difference? Why were there no thoughts in the first example and thoughts in the second one?

In the first example when asked to tell me about food in general no or few thoughts came to mind because food in general is not something we desire. Food in general is something that we must eat in order to survive. Food to eat in general is not something that we think we can find unconditional pleasure in doing. As a result, there is no desire for food in general and consequently no thoughts came to your mind about it.

However, in the second example when I asked you specifically about your "favorite food," something different happened didn't it? Favorites generally become favorites because of a "desire" for them. You taste a new food today that you have never eaten. You "like" it. Now that you like it, you then "desire" to have it again. Now when asked about a favorite food, this new desire acts like a seed planted in the soil of your unconscious mind which germinates and sprouts forth as a thought about it. Now you have a "thought" about this food which all happened based on the original desire.

The process is the same in the case of something that you do not like. Desire "for" something is no different for desire to "not" have something else. They both act as seeds planted in the soil of the mind and spring forth as thoughts about that thing.

The knowledge of the affect that desire plays in our lives is important to understand for everyone. It is especially important for the person who wants to study ancient mystical spirituality. Without the knowledge of how desire operates in our lives, it is easy to think that we are subject to the myriad number of thoughts that we regularly have. Knowledge that every thought we have ever had, about anything, has its origins in a specific desire that we had previously does an important thing. ***It lets us know how we can control our thoughts!*** Knowing that desire actually creates thoughts means that our ability to control thoughts can directly be influenced by "actively" determining what we desire. Instead of leaving desire to chance which is what many people do, conscious decisions of "what" to desire can be created. When we control what we desire, we control what we will have thoughts about in the future.

I have yet to meet a person who has the ability to literally tell their mind what to think about or what not to think about it. This does not mean that this type of person does not exist. However, this type of practice is not a common one. Until this ability is developed, we can instead do the next best thing which is to control the process. For you as a spiritual aspirant, this is big. Now you can control your thoughts like precept number one above says by controlling your desires. Desire for Nehast in this lifetime will turn into thoughts about how this goal will be achieved. Elimination of desire for things outside of this goal can be eliminated and consequently thoughts about these outside things can be curtailed and then eliminated also. As actions generally follow thoughts, control of what you desire will simultaneously allow you to control both your thoughts and actions. Adherence to the remaining eight precepts will be much easier once these first two are mastered.

Mastery in understanding the place "desire" has in the life of the spiritual aspirant and its importance cannot be stressed enough.

Belief

The second quality to cultivate that can be found in an authentic aspirant is "belief" in the teachings. Combine this with "belief" that their practice of them will produce the same result for you that it has for others and the result is achievement of Nehast in this lifetime. The "belief" that you can achieve your "desires" is important whatever goal you may have in life. This is true also in the practice of authentic spirituality. Three of the initiatic precepts above speak directly about "belief" on the spiritual path.

1. "Have faith in your master's ability to lead you along the path of truth,"
2. "Have faith in your own ability to accept the truth,"
3. "Have faith in your ability to act with wisdom,"

Faith is belief in something that has not been experienced. Faith/belief is supposed to be a short term practice until one "experiences" what was at first "believed." Without experience faith is blind and can do much damage to a person. Once "experienced" there is no longer anything to believe as now what was believed in is now "known." In time what is "known" leads to intuitional knowledge.

On its face, believing in something until you get the experience to know it does not seem like something difficult to do. However the personality of a person operates in such a way that belief in certain things is a difficult thing to do.

For example you have probably heard the phrase "think positive." You might even "believe" that thinking positive is a good thing to do. Although you may at times say the words "think positive," this does not mean that deep down inside you really "believe" that thinking positive will have any effect on your life.

It is a common practice in this day and time to orally "say" they believe something but unconsciously they don't. This is the main problem with the concept of believing. This is especially true about believing in those things that we cannot experience through our senses. Hence the phrase "seeing is believing." An argument can be made that this is the reason why there are so many disenchanted and unfulfilled people. All they "see" are other disenchanted and unfulfilled people so their experience tells them that this is all that exists. Even the so called "happy" people, those with money and fame have many issues. We "see" them experiencing a variety and multitude of problems. So belief in something other than what is seen every day (the unknown to the senses) is difficult to overcome.

Relating belief to authentic spirituality is another thing altogether. Here you as an aspirant are being asked to believe in the teachings, your teacher, and yourself. The belief in all three is that their practice will result in your obtainment of spiritual awakening (Nehast). Although this is simple, this is not an easy thing to do. One of the Kamitic Proverbs speaks on why this is so.

"It is very hard; to leave the things we have grown used to, which meet our gaze on every side. Appearances delight us, whereas the things that appear not make their believing hard. Evils are the more apparent things, whereas the good (Divine) can never show itself unto the eyes, for it hath neither form nor figure."

Belief as a concept can better be understood when it is realized that belief is a part of a process that leads to experience and knowing. It is like a bridge that leads from one place to another. The problem is that it is easy to have a seat on the bridge, camp out there, and forget what the destination is. This is what happens when a person has blind faith. They have camped out on the bridge and forgotten both where they have come from and where they are going. Belief is supposed to lead you somewhere to a destination. It is not a place to reside in.

"An Aspirant's Guide To Practicing The Egyptian Mysteries"

Belief in the teachings of an authentic spiritual practice, teacher and yourself is the bridge leading you away from the past experiences of *the "things we have grown used to, which meet our gaze on every side,"* spoken in the proverb above, to the experience of *"the good (Divine) which can never show itself unto the eyes"* (Word added). Keep this in mind and "belief" in things will become your friend and aid you in your quest. Forget about this and you will become content to go nowhere while thinking that you have arrived.

Spiritual Vigilance

The third quality of an authentic aspirant to be cultivated is spiritual vigilance. Vigilance at all times of your thoughts and actions is very important on the spiritual path. You must be aware of every thought that goes into or comes out of your mind because negative impressions create mental blocks which slow spiritual evolution and realization.

Anpu represents the aspect of your personality that "watches" what enters into your unconscious mind and most importantly keeps out that which does not belong. When the Anpu faculty is working properly, your conscious mind acts like a gatekeeper of a facility does. A gatekeeper only lets those who belong in an area entry into it. He/she keeps out all others who do not belong there. The Anpu faculty in a person is their conscious mind. This is the aspect of a person that tells them not to eat that food that's not good for them, or not to drink things harmful to it. Everyone has this Anpu faculty. The difference is that some people have a trained faculty and the willpower to act in accordance with it tells them. The rest allow their ego/emotions to rule them and they instead become entangled in numerous unhealthy situations.

Few people realize that there are certain things that simply do not belong in their unconscious mind. They have allowed the "gatekeeper" aspect of their personality to fall asleep on the job. What happens when a facility gatekeeper falls asleep on the job? Others break into the facility and do terrible things. Robbers, thieves and those with evil intentions once inside, wreak havoc on the place. Robbers and thieves allowed into the unconscious part of our minds do the same thing. They wreak havoc in our lives. This is the cause of heartache, pain, and frustration in a person's life. There is an Ancient Egyptian Christian text called the Gospel of Thomas that speaks directly about this.

From the Gospel of Thomas:

25. If the master of the house knows that the thief is coming, he will watch before he comes and will not allow him to force entry into his royal house to carry off its furniture. You then be on the watch against the world. Gird your loins with great energy, so that the brigands (bandits) do not find any way of reaching you, for they find any place you fail to watch.

107. Jesus says: "Blessed is the man who knows where the robbers are going to enter, so that he watches, he gathers his belongings and girds his loins before they enter."

The house here refers to your unconscious mind and the thief represents negative personality characteristics such as anger, hate, greed, selfishness etc. Once these negative characteristics make it past your gatekeeper into your house (your unconscious mind), they cloud your vision of the Soul (oneness). The Self, the innermost essence of every person will "save" you once you turn to the Self as the only reality. This turning to the Self instead of indulging in the egoism of the mind destroys the possibility of any danger in the realm of time and space or in the Astral Planes. This is what Jesus was referring to when he spoke about guarding against robbers who are egoism, ignorance, anger, hate, and lust just to name a few. When you are "watchful" for these negative emotional states there can be no surprise. In fact when you are ready for them, it is easy to overcome them. However for the person who is not on the lookout for them, they always "unexpectedly" pop up which often leads to a negative surprise and unexpected tragedy.

This is unfortunate because this way of living life makes the robbers (egoism, ignorance anger etc.) normal parts of your life. All of a sudden you begin to believe that is normal to be angry. All of a sudden you begin to believe it is normal to lust. Selfishness, jealousy, envy and greed, just to name a few, become normal aspects of everyday life common to everyone. In fact you hear people who believe such things make comments like "being upset or angry is a part of being human," and/or "controlling all aspects of your personality is not even human!" Egoism, ignorance and the other negative personality traits become the reality and this view prevents this person from experiencing the oneness of Creation and of the Divine.

In short spiritual vigilance is the process of consciously being aware of every thought that enters into your unconscious mind. This consciousness makes it easier to simultaneously allow in and keep out certain images and information. Images and information that assist you on the spiritual path are to be allowed in. The wisdom teachings, parables, songs, reflection and meditation are information to be allowed into your unconscious mind as these purify and allow it to expand in consciousness. Gossip, idle chatter, watching killing, and lustful sex to name a few, open the doorway to the robbers of anger, jealousy, greed and the others just spoken of. This type of information is to be kept out of your unconscious mind as they constrict consciousness.

Good Association

Good Association is the fourth quality to be cultivated by an authentic aspirant. Have you ever heard any of the following phrases?

1. "Birds of a feather flock together!"
2. "Great minds think alike!"
3. "It takes one to know one!"
4. "Game peeps game!"

In Ancient times, good association consisted of interaction and study in the Temple with the Sages and Saints. There the aspirant was able to learn and receive the wisdom teachings in an unobstructed way. Then the aspirant would leave the Temple for periods of time and practice what they had learned about self-control when confronted with everyday worldly minded people. The Temple was the place where the initiate could go on a regular basis to receive instruction and counseling on the correct application of the teachings in day to day to life.

Good Association is important because people tend to emulate and mock others they associate with. Birds of a feather flock together because they have things in common. So keeping yourself around people who have the qualities that you seek keeps the teachings at the forefront of your mind.

In its highest sense, Good Association consists of a teacher-disciple relationship where the yogic teachings of spirituality are presented by the teacher to the student. Through continuous association with the preceptor, sage or other spiritually advanced personality, the authentic aspirant is led to discover his/her true spiritual identity.

Today we don't have Temples like those of yester year. Nor do we have many authentic Preceptors, Sages and Saints. Today we have to make adjustments so that we can still associate with those advanced personality types. This can be done by taking part in the activities that these people have. If the Preceptor, Sage or Teacher has radio or television broadcasts, listen to them. If they have regular meetings or Conferences go to them. Have conversations with them and their advanced students by calling them and talking to them on a regular basis. This is how "Good Association" can be practiced today.

Conversely you can also practice Good Association by limiting your interactions with worldly minded people. For clarity sake a worldly person is someone who thinks that it is normal to "not" be in control of their personality. Those people with personalities that are continuously affected by anger, hate, greed, lust, impulsiveness and selfishness, is detrimental to the mental peace of an aspirant, especially a beginning practitioner of the teachings. Those personality types who are constantly on the go, constantly arguing and constantly agitated are afflicted with intense identification with their bodies and senses. These people are unaware of their divine nature. Interactions with these personality types are anything but "good" and are to be limited.

Watching television and listening to the radio, unless they are programs that discuss the practices that lead to spiritual realization, is an example of "Poor" Association and should curtailed at worst and avoided at best. Watching television when you're glued to it promotes dullness of the mind and this leads to spiritual insensitivity.

The goal of Good Association is to lead you to having a state of mind which is tranquil, peaceful, and contented. This is the mind an authentic aspirant strives to have.

Understanding the Difference between Sublimation of Negative Emotions and Suppression of Them

Although what follows is not what I refer to as a "quality" of an authentic aspirant, an authentic aspirant would be wise to heed the lessons and advice that will soon follow.

If you have not heard it, you will soon discover that on the path to awakening to the higher spiritual reality, the teachings discuss the importance of learning how to sublimate negative personality characteristics. The information presented is the answer to a question given by Dr. Karen Clark Ashby (Seba Dja) about the difference between sublimating one negative emotion, anger, and suppressing it. The advice given can be applied to any negative personality characteristic and should be used in your own spiritual practice.

Question:
On the show this past Saturday regarding Overcoming Anger, you mentioned that there is a difference between "suppressing" anger and "sublimating" it.

Would you clarify what this difference is and how it applies to our practice of the teachings?

Answer by Dr. Karen Ashby (Seba Dja):
"Yes, there is a difference between "suppressing" anger and "sublimating" it.

In Shetaut Neter, the emphasis of how to handle negative emotions is on sublimation of those negative emotions, rather than on suppression of emotions such as anger.

However, in dealing with anger, suppression may be (and is often) applied initially…but only initially. It is a short term stop gap measure when one does not have a higher capacity to not get angry, but then the energy of that anger has to go somewhere, and if it is not transformed into something more useful and positive or vented in some way, it will internally build until, as we generally say, the person explodes, meaning they have an overly emotionally or and hysterical outburst.

Suppression just means repressing one's emotions and feelings, keeping them in. So, just suppression alone cannot eliminate negative emotions such as anger. Even western psychology is aware that it is not healthy to just suppress your anger. They suggest it is better to get it out, but in a healthy way. So they may teach ways of calming down (the yogic techniques of deep breathing and relaxation are being incorporated more and more into mainstream psychology) and ways that you can dissipate the energy without hurting anyone. You can go and punch a pillow or beat a bean bag, etc., to get out your frustration without hurting anyone. And this latter approach is helpful…to a degree, for worldly persons. It keeps them "normal" accord ding to normal worldly standards.

But with suppression, the negative ariu (mental impressions of anger), the ariu that allowed the negative emotion to erupt, is not being dealt with. Take someone who is racist or sexist or homophobic. If they are at work or in a public setting where they know it is unacceptable to express their sentiments of anger at seeing "these people" taking over the country, they will suppress their emotion of anger, and may go home and punch a wall or a tree or yell and scream or do whatever to vent their anger. So the energy has been released, but there is no spiritual transformation in the personality. The person still remains a racist/sexist or homophobe. There is no positive spiritual evolution. Rather, the negative ariu has become more intensified by the expression of anger and hate.

Sublimation on the other and is a means of redirecting the energy in a manner that it will facilitate one's spiritual evolution. Have you ever been angry at someone for something, but then when you get to a deeper understanding of the issue, you find out that the person you were angry at was not the cause of the situation that elicited your anger, and your anger dissipated, or that her/his story diffused your anger, and perhaps also made you feel a little guilty of even being angry in the first place? Perhaps your friend was supposed to meet you somewhere for an appointment, and did not show up. You became angry with her, but then later on found out she was in an accident and had to go to the hospital. In this case, a deeper understanding of the situation allowed the anger to dissipate, and a portion of it to be sublimated into the feelings of compassion for your friend and feelings of guilt about having become angry in the first place (your conscience). With deeper insight, you may learn to not jump to a conclusion each time someone disappoints you, because maybe they have a valid reason. So, even in practical life, allowing understanding to overcome misunderstanding is a means of slowly effacing the negative mental impressions, the ariu, but this process can take lifetimes if it is not part of an intensive mystical-spiritual movement to attain Nehast, Enlightenment. Imagine how much more potent the cleansing of ariu will be if it has the force of understanding of your true essence (Higher Self) behind it, overcoming the greatest misunderstanding, that you are not the wave-like ego-personality, but in fact the ocean-like Divine Self.

The Shedy disciplines are thus the most effective means of sublimating the negative energies and cleansing the negative ariu. Negative energies, like anger, are just disbalanced or dis-harmonious energies. The shedy disciplines balance and harmonize those negative energies. The shedy disciplines work at the different levels of mind, which include the astral and causal bodies (the subtle spiritual bodies), to purify the ariu of anger in the subconscious and unconscious mind as well as increase your self-restraint and self-control, and also makes you more detached, and thus, less reactive. The more you unleash the positive in you through the practice of the Shedy disciplines, the more the negative egoistic traits will vanish from your personality. Further, through the Shedy disciplines, you are working to remove the very source of the negative emotions, egoism."

"An Aspirant's Guide To Practicing The Egyptian Mysteries"

SECTION I

I Found It! This Is It!
(Shetaut Neter)

The chapters in this section provide information about what can be expected around the initial time that a person chooses Shetaut Neter to be their path towards spiritual enlightenment (Nehast). What we unconsciously expect from ourselves and others as a result of this choice is explored. For me what actually happened was far different from what I thought would occur. These chapters, once read, will assist you in your daily walk as they better reflect what actually happens when practicing the disciplines day to day than mental notions of what we would like those experiences to be.

Much of the information provided is based upon my actual experiences since I began my own daily practice of Shetaut Neter.

"An Aspirant's Guide To Practicing The Egyptian Mysteries"

NEBERDJER

The All Encompassing Divinity

"Do Not Allow What You Think or How You Think to LIMIT What You Think or How You Think!"

By: Anpu Waset

"An Aspirant's Guide To Practicing The Egyptian Mysteries"

Shetaut Neter
(Secrets about the Divine Self)

Chapter 1

I FOUND IT! THIS IS IT!

Discovering a teaching that leads to Enlightenment is often very exciting. As a reader of these words you can probably identify with this statement. For some people the discovery of Shetaut Neter, or another ancient mystical tradition, creates a "euphoric feeling." This should not be surprising as the thrill of finding the means towards spiritual emancipation for many is nothing short of fantastic. There are those who want to share their new philosophical and religious teachings with everyone in their family. These teachings are also shared with those people in their inner circle. At the beginning the "teachings" often wind up being the only thing being discussed. If this has happened to you or is happening currently rest assured that this is quite normal.

This "euphoric feeling" is like a form of energy. If channeled properly, this energy will act like a form of fuel which will propel your spiritual practice. Vehicles need fuel to function. You as a new practitioner of the teachings will need fuel to practice the teachings on a daily basis. This fuel/energy feeds your will power. It is will power that is needed to consistently practice something. If channeled improperly though, it can be a cause of frustration and discouragement.

<u>Purification</u>

One of the reasons that the "euphoric this is it feeling!" is present is because at our core we have longed for the union between our lower and higher consciousness. With the discovery of Shetaut Neter, we intuitively know that this path will lead us to this union. But what specifically do we need to do which will lead to this union? We must purify every aspect of our personality thru what is known as the Integrated Practice of Yoga.

<u>Why Do We Need To Purify Ourselves?</u>

Purification of our personality is necessary because we have mistakenly believed for many lifetimes that we are something other than what we are. We have believed an idea that is not true. Many people unconsciously believe that we are human beings having intermittent spiritual experiences. In actuality the opposite is true. We are spiritual beings having an intermittent human experience. This is the main reason that the union between our lower consciousness and higher consciousness has not occurred. We think we are separated from the Divine/God as opposed to being connected with the Divine at this and every moment. Union cannot occur until this belief is eradicated. (Purified)

What Specifically Needs To Be Purified?

The aim of the Shetaut Neter practices is to purify both the outer and inner aspects of the personality. The outer personality consists of your ego/personality. This is the make believe idea of who you think you are. For most people this idea is limited to the belief that we are individuals in the midst of other individuals who are all separate from each other. This idea leads to greed, jealousy, envy, lust conditional love, frustration and a host of other ills. It is a mental creation developed by people when they stop seeing themselves as one with the Divine and instead believe that they are separate entities apart from God and Creation.

Purification is also necessary for the inner aspect of our being. The inner aspect consists of our mind which dwells in what is known as the astral plane. This subtle inner aspect of our being also believes that it is something that it is not. The mind has grown accustomed to accepting as "real" data given to it by our senses. We have grown to believe that everything that we taste, touch, hear, see and smell is the full extent of reality. But this way of thinking is mistaken because the senses do not provide accurate reflections of existence. The concept of reality would be much different if we could see like a hawk and hear like a dog.

As a result of accepting this skewed view of reality, our minds now seek union with objects in time and space and wait for death to occur to fully know and have union with God. This aspect of the purification process is the most subtle and depending upon your level of spiritual evolution may require the most discipline. A mind filled with the outlandish notions of individuality and separateness prevents a person from achieving spiritual union. However, the mind once purified and cleansed of these ideas, is the vehicle by which spiritual realization can occur.

How Is This Done?

Purification of the entire mind body complex is done thru the practice of the Shetaut Neter disciplines which are known as the integrated practice of Yoga. To properly explain this process, some words need to be defined for clarity.

SHETAUT NETER

"An Aspirant's Guide To Practicing The Egyptian Mysteries"

"SHETAUT" AS THE FIRST WORD MEANS **SECRET** OR **HIDDEN** OR **MYSTERY**. "NETER" AS THE SECOND WORD MEANS **DIVINITY**. "SHETAUT NETER" THEREFORE MEANS THE TEACHING ABOUT THE SECRET, HIDDEN "SUPREME BEING," OR "DIVINE MYSTERIES." FOR A DETAILED EXPOSITION ON NETERIANISM, SEE THE BOOK "EGYPTIAN MYSTERIES VOLUME 1 BY DR. MUATA ASHBY.

SHETI

SHETI COMES FROM THE ROOT WORD "SHETAUT" WHICH AS STATED ABOVE MEANS **SECRET, HIDDEN, OR UNKNOWN** OR THAT WHICH CANNOT BE SEEN THRU OR UNDERSTOOD. SOMETHING WHICH IS A **SECRET** OR **MYSTERY**.

SHETI THEREFORE ARE THE **PRACTICES** AND **DISCIPLINES WHICH** LEAD A PERSON TO "**DISCOVER**" THAT WHICH IS **HIDDEN, SECRET,** OR **UNKNOWN** WHICH IS THE **UNDERLYING BASIS** OF ALL OF CREATION.

SHETI "PRACTICES

ANY PRACTICE OR DISCIPLINE WHICH HELPS A PERSON DISCOVER THAT WHICH IS "HIDDEN" AND "SECRET" IS A SHETI PRACTICE. INHERENT IN THE PRACTICE HOWEVER IS THE UNDERSTANDING THAT A PERSON'S IGNORANCE OF THEIR HIGHER NATURE AND SELF IS AN IMPEDIMENT TO KNOWING THAT WHICH IS "HIDDEN." TO UNDERSTAND THE TEACHINGS WHICH ALLOW A PERSON TO "KNOW" THAT WHICH IS "HIDDEN" REQUIRES THAT A PERSON'S MIND/EGO BECOME PURIFIED OR CLEANSED. BOTH MUST BE PURIFIED AND CLEANSED OF THE CONSCIOUS, SUBCONSCIOUS AND UNCONSCIOUS IMPRESSIONS THAT HAVE A PERSON BELIEVE THAT THEY ARE SOEMTHING OTHER THAN THE TRUTH. MOST PEOPLE BELIEVE THAT THEY ARE PHYSICAL BEINGS HAVING INTERMITTENT SPIRITUAL EXPERIENCES. HOWEVER, THE OPPOSITE IS IN FACT THE TRUTH. WE ARE SPIRITUAL BEINGS HAVING AN INTERMITTENT PHYSICAL EXPERIENCE! UNTIL THERE IS A CERTAIN LEVEL OF CLEANSING OF THE CONSCIOUS, SUBCONSCIOUS AND UNCONSCIOUS IMPRESSIONS THAT HAVE US BELIEVE WE ARE THE BODY, THE ABILITY TO "FULLY" UNDERSTAND THE DEEPER ASPECTS OF THE TEACHING WILL BE LIMITED. SHETI PRACTICES ARE

THEREFORE THE MEANS BY WHICH THIS CLEANSING/PURIFICATION OCCURS. IN OUR TRADITION, THERE ARE FOUR MAIN DISCIPLINES WHICH MADE UP AND CONSTITUTED THAT WHICH WAS KNOWN AS THE "MYSTERIES." THE MYSTERIES ARE WHAT WAS TAUGHT IN THE TEMPLES OF KEMET AND ARE ALSO KNOWN AS THE INTEGRATED PRACTICE OF YOGA. THE "MYSTERIES" ARE KNOWN AS THE **SHETI OF DEVOTION, SHETI OF MEDITATION, SHETI OF WISDOM, AND SHETI OF ACTION (MAAT).**

WHAT ARE THE EVERYDAY DISCIPLINES NEEDED TO CONDUCT A SHETI "PRACTICE"?

BEFORE DISCUSSING THE DISCIPLINES RELATED TO SHETI, IT MUST BE CLEARLY UNDERSTOOD THAT THE SAGES OF KEMET TAUGHT THAT THE EGO/PERSONALITY OF ALL PEOPLE IS COMPOSED OF FOUR ASPECTS:

1. INTELLECT.
2. EMOTIONS.
3. WILL.
4. PHYSICAL BODY.

THEY BELIEVED THAT EACH ASPECT OF THE EGO/PERSONALITY CREATES CONSCIOUS, SUBCONSCIOUS AND UNCONSCIOUS IMPRESSIONS IN THE MIND WHICH AFFIRM AND REAFFIRM THE BELIEF THAT PEOPLE ARE NOTHING MORE THAN THE "BODY." EACH SHETI PRACTICE WAS DESIGNED TO PURIFY/CLEANSE THAT SPECIFIC ASPECT OF THE PERSONALITY/EGO. THE SIMULTANEOUS CLEANSING OF EACH ASPECT WAS/IS KNOWN AS THE "INTEGRATED PRACTICE OF YOGA."

A. SHETI OF WISDOM (INTELLECT)

THE SHETI OF WISDOM IS THE PROCESS OF STUDYING THE HIGHEST TEACHINGS, (THE WISDOM TEXTS AND WRITINGS OF SAGES AND SAINTS) AND THEN REFLECTING AND MEDITATING ON THEM. THIS SHETI PRACTICE PURIFIES/CLEANSES THE "INTELLECT" OF IMPRESSIONS THAT THE BODY AND THAT WHICH APPEAR TO BE REAL THROUGH THE SENSES IS THE FULLEST EXTENT OF CREATION.

B. SHETI OF DEVOTION (EMOTIONS)

EVERYONE HAS A NEED TO LOVE AND BE LOVED. THIS OFTENTIMES MANIFESTS THRU US BY WAY OF OUR EMOTIONS. ANYONE WHO HAS EVER FALLEN IN LOVE IS AWARE THAT THERE IS A LOT OF ENERGY INVOLVED IN THIS STATE OF BEING. WHEN IN LOVE, PEOPLE SOMETIMES CANNOT EAT, SLEEP OR EVEN DRINK BECAUSE THEY ARE THINKING ABOUT THAT SPECIAL PERSON OR OBJECT OF THEIR AFFECTION. PHYSIOLOGICALLY MANY CHANGES OCCUR IN THE BODY. THE HEART RATE, BLOOD PRESSURE, AND OTHERS CHANGE WHEN A PERSON HAS THIS "FEELING." UNFORTUNATELY, NEGATIVE IMPRESSIONS ARE FORMED IN THE MIND WHEN A PERSON SEEKS LOVE FROM PEOPLE/OBJECTS IN THE WORLD. THE PERSON BEGINS TO THINK THAT THE PERSON/OBJECT (OR THE "*RIGHT PERSON OR OBJECT*") WILL MAKE THEM HAPPY.

WHAT IS NOT REALIZED BY PEOPLE IS THAT WHAT THEY ARE ACTUALLY BEING ATTRACTED TO IS THE "***HIDDEN, SECRET, UNKNOWN***" UNDERLYING ASPECT SPOKEN OF EARLIER IN THE PERSON THEY ARE IN LOVE WITH. IN EFFECT YOU ARE ATTRACTED TO THE "GOD/SELF" IN THEM WHICH YOU JUST SO HAPPEN TO BE BETTER AT SEEING IN THEM THAN IN OTHERS.

THE SHETI OF DEVOTION HAS AS ITS GOAL THE PURIFICATION OF THE EMOTIONS BY DIRECTING THIS ENERGY AWAY FROM THE "OUTER PHYSICAL BODY" OF A PERSON TO THE UNDERLYING BASIS IN THEM WHICH YOU ARE ACTUALLY ATTRACTED TO.

C. SHETI OF MEDITATION (WILL)

EVERYONE HAS A WILL. THE PRACTICE OF MEDITATION STRENGTHENS THE WILL POWER OF A PERSON. THE PRACTICE ALSO CLEANSES THE SUBCONSCIOUS AND UNCONSCIOUS IMPRESSIONS IN THE MIND WHICH HAVE A PERSON BELIEVE THEY ARE THE BODY. IN THE ADVANCED STAGES, MEDITATION ALLOWS A PERSON TO "EXPERIENCE" THEMSELVES AS THE HIGHER ASPECT OF THEIR BEING.

D. SHETI OF RIGHTEOUS ACTION

"An Aspirant's Guide To Practicing The Egyptian Mysteries"

EVERYTHING THAT A PERSON DOES OCCURS THROUGH SOME TYPE OF ACTION. EVEN THOUGHTS THEMSELVES ARE ACTIONS. ALL ACTIONS ONCE PERFORMED LEAVE IMPRESSIONS IN THE MIND. IMPRESSIONS CAN BE LIKENED TO FEELINGS. YOU DO THIS ACT, YOU FEEL GOOD. YOU DO SOMETHING ELSE YOU FEEL BAD AND SO ON. HOWEVER, MOST ACTIONS ARE DONE FROM THE PERSPECTIVE THAT WE ARE THE BODY. SO A CONSTANT CONFIRMATION OF US BEING A BODY IS GIVEN THRU OUR ACTIONS ON A SECOND BY SECOND BASIS.

THE SHETI OF RIGHTEOUS ACTION HAS A PERSON ENGAGE IN ACTIONS THAT HELP HIM/HER TO SEE THEM AS INFINITE, IMMORTAL ETC. THE RIGHTOUS ACTIONS IN OUR TRADITION ARE THE MAAT PRECEPTS. THEY ARE 42 IN NUMBER. LIVING YOUR LIFE ON A DAILY BASIS THRU THE "PRACTICE" OF THESE PRECEPTS WILL PURIFY THE EGO.

The integrated Sheti practice purifies every aspect of the personality in a balanced and harmonious way.

"An Aspirant's Guide To Practicing The Egyptian Mysteries"

Discernment and Discriminative Knowledge of What is Real and What is Not Real.

"An Aspirant's Guide To Practicing The Egyptian Mysteries"

(Purification of the heart)

Chapter 2

Congratulate Yourself & Trust The Process!

Now that you have decided to embark on the spiritual path, one thing that will assist you in your walk is to learn how to treat yourself throughout this process. Although many in society find it easy to focus on mistakes made when things happen, this type of mindset does not benefit a spiritual practice. Your spiritual growth will be enhanced if you develop the ability to increase your positive spiritual moments while minimizing your negative ones. This can be done by learning how to congratulate yourself on a regular basis when your spiritual practice warrants it. Affirmation and trust of the purification process, puts you in a position to succeed on the spiritual path.

Effort should be made to recognize every spiritual accomplishment done every moment. Learning how to recognize and be proud of these victories is important. As victories build up, so does willpower. In time, this willpower will combine with wisdom and devotion to become a force so strong that spiritual awakening becomes assured. This is true for the new practitioner. This is also true for the person who has studied the teachings for years.

There is a saying that goes "with friends like these who needs enemies?" Quite often we as people can be our own worst enemies. The tendency in many of us is to highlight our shortcomings and minimize our achievements. Ultimately our goal is balance when dealing with both aspects of our personalities. However balance is not the norm for many of us. The common tendency for many of us is one sided on the side of being negative. Often it takes an outsider such as a spouse, friend or relative to point out the fact that we are being critical to ourselves. To achieve balance under these one sided negative circumstances we need to err on the side of being positive with ourselves and accomplishments.

This means that a concerted effort should be made to congratulate yourself every time you do something in harmony with your spiritual practice. Pat yourself on the back when you do your Sheti practice in the morning. Smile and be proud of yourself when you resist the temptation to eat that piece of chocolate cake. Give yourself a high five when you hold your tongue and not curse in a situation you normally would curse in. Allow yourself to feel good when you see the Divine in a flower or cloud. These are large accomplishments worthy of praise. When combined together over a period of time, they create new impressions (ari) which purify us from the belief that we are nothing more than the body.

As a new aspirant, it is easy to practice the teachings within the first year or two of discovering them. Excitement about them during this time is very high. You could say that you have a consistent adrenaline rush as you may experience a constant euphoric feeling. This is normal and is a good thing. During this time the Integrated Yoga Practice of Shetaut Neter combined with the three fold daily worship program will be easily maintained. But keep in mind that the euphoric feeling time frame will not last. This phase will subside and if the aspirant is not aware may easily result in a victory for our ego which in our tradition is known as Set.

The ego/Set will begin to win victories as this phase ends because the tendency of the aspirant will be to start judging their spiritual progress and practice of the teachings. This is a dangerous time and will be noticed when the following type of comments are made.

1. *"Why did I do that? I shouldn't still be doing things like that?"*
2. *"I still want that car but I should be over that desire by now!"*
3. *"The ladies still look good to me. Sages don't see women like this!"*
4. *"I've been studying the teachings now for 3-4 years and don't see any improvement.*
5. *"I still get lonely. I should be beyond this by now."*
6. *"I still get upset. My practice must be off."*
7. *"My ex-spouse still gets on my nerves. The teachings must not be working for me."*
8. *"My current spouse is getting on my nerves. I must not be practicing the teachings correctly."*
9. *"I practice the teachings everyday and my finances are still a mess. I am barely taking care of myself. Has the Divine left me? Is my practice out of order? At some point my financial picture should have improved by now."*
10. *"The teachings say I don't need a mate to be complete and whole. But I want one. What's wrong with me?"*

After this initial euphoric phase, it will be easy to begin judging how well we are doing with our Sheti Practice. However upon reflection we find that this judging is quite laughable because of who is doing the judging. Once studied closely we find that it is our ego/Set doing the judging. Think about this for a moment. Our ego/Set, which is what we are purifying, is measuring our spiritual progress. Keep in mind that the purification process basically removes the ego/Set from the

prominent position of authority as ruler over Kamit. So the aspect of us that knows that its time is close to expiration now has a new set of keys to keep it in the driver's seat. It is now telling you how well you are doing to remove it.

Needless to say, the ego will not give us an unbiased opinion of this movement. It has everything to gain and nothing to lose by giving us biased opinions of ourselves. You can see how unpreparedness for this situation could be the means by which much spiritual frustration can occur.

With planning and foresight, this occurrence can be readily dealt with and even negated altogether. The Ancient Egyptian Christian text mentioned earlier provides guidance on this issue.

From the Gospel of Thomas:

> **25. If the master of the house knows that the thief is coming, he will watch before he comes and will not allow him to force an entry into his royal house to carry off its furniture. You can then be on the watch against the world. Gird your loins with great energy, so that the brigands (bandits) do not find any way of reaching you; for they find any place you fail to watch.**
>
> **107. Jesus says: "Blessed is the man who knows where the robbers are going to enter, so that he watches, he gathers his belongings and girds his loins before they enter.**

Awareness of what to expect is the key. Those who are able to mentally be aware of the robbers and thieves of anger, hate, greed, selfishness etc., will not allow those to enter into their house (unconscious mind) and cloud their vision of the Soul (oneness). However, this takes much mental discipline and practice. It also takes a lot of time and energy being in a "watchful" state. For many of us, this advanced practice is not practical in our daily life. One thing that we can more easily do as beginning practitioners (1-4 years as aspirants) is become our own cheering section and cheerleader around our practice of the teachings.

Consider the implementation of a reward system in your spiritual practice life. One way to do this is by developing a number of rewards that you like that are in harmony with the spiritual practice itself. For example many people like natural fruit smoothies. They taste good and are also good for the body. EVERY time you do something in the course of your day that promotes your spiritual movement, congratulate yourself and reward yourself with a smoothie. While you prepare it, smile and reflect on what you accomplished. As you drink it, pat yourself on the back and appreciate the willpower you exhibited in doing the positive action.

Reward yourself like this for EVERY positive action that you do. After a short period of time, you will find that your positive actions will grow large in number. At this point you may run out of rewards for each action. At that point consider keeping a tally of the number of actions and then begin rewarding yourself at the end of the day or week for a certain number of accumulated positive actions. Develop a reward for each number and reward yourself accordingly. Do this while you maintain the same sense of fanfare while congratulating yourself constantly. You might say something like, "I already have 15 positive spiritual actions in less than two days. By the end of the week I know I will have 50 and will be able to go to dinner at the Live Food restaurant!" Keep up the fanfare and be your best cheerleader.

Simultaneous with this praise should be the minimization of those acts which would provide evidence of failure of practicing the teachings. Behaviors which you believe contradict the teachings and your conscience. Everyone knows when they do something wrong. When these times come DO NOT make a big deal out of it. Look over it and don't give it much thought. Reflect on what happened but do not dwell on it. Seek to find the cause of the error and resolve it so that the next time this situation occurs you will be able to overcome it. Shift your consciousness. The more you congratulate yourself on your good works and deeds while simultaneously resolving the cause of the negatives, the more you will unconsciously gravitate towards doing more righteous things. As you affirm your good works in this way, the mind will assert more willpower over the ego and will unconsciously move you towards doing more of these righteous types of actions until this way of living becomes the norm for you.

Ultimately, your mind cannot help but to make you internally feel good about your spiritual movement when you begin realizing that your positive actions far outweigh your negative ones. If practiced in this way, this internal good feeling will stay with you.

Trust the Process!

Evaluating progress on the spiritual path cannot be done with methods we are accustomed to in the world. Beware of setting goals for a spiritual practice based upon ideas from the world. Typically people set goals when there is something that they want to achieve. "I want to have a job making $75, 000 dollars in two years," is an example of a goal that a person might make. Measuring progress in this example is easy because you know where you are when you begin and where you want to be in a specific time period. However, spiritual growth on the path cannot be measured in this way.

Spiritual practices are implemented as a process to purify the mind, body and soul of a person so that they can realize their oneness with the Divine. (Nehast) It is a process that is short for some and long for others as everyone has different levels of purification that are needed. The best thing that can be done is to TRUST THE PROCESS!

The Sages of Ancient Kamit developed the Mystery Schools and the Sheti practices developed within them over thousands of years. Their methods were well tested, tried and true. The Sheti practices restated in the books by the Sema Institute of Yoga are no different today than they were thousands of years ago. It has been stated by Sebai Maa and Seba Dja that practice on the path results in spiritual liberation in this lifetime for the aspirant who practices the teachings without fail. So success is assured. So do not attempt to measure success on the path in the traditional sense.

You will become a calmer person. You will become more peaceful. Negative aspects of your personality will fall away in degrees. So over periods of days, weeks, or maybe even months, you may not notice anything different about yourself even though you are practicing the teachings diligently. No matter what keep going, congratulate yourself and trust the process. Remember it works for every aspirant who practices the teachings without fail!

"An Aspirant's Guide To Practicing The Egyptian Mysteries"

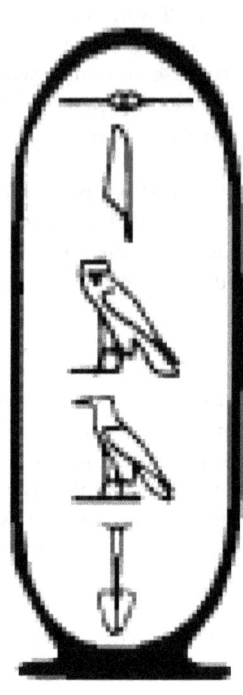

Chapter 3

General Considerations of the Impact of YOUR study of the Teachings on Members of Your Family

This chapter presents common scenarios that will occur as discussion about the teachings is made to your inner circle of family and friends. The intent is to provide an overview of what to expect when this happens. These members will NOT react the same way when hearing about the teachings as you did when you first heard them.

It would be both prudent and wise for you to consider the fact that your family and friends may initially be against your new practice. A central reason for this stance is that this new study will change the nature of their relationship with you. From the perspective of family members and friends, prior to your study and practice of Shetaut Neter, you were a particular type of person acting a particular type of way. This "old you" is the person who they know, love and have grown accustomed to. Your wife or husband married this "other" person. Your children grew up with this "other" person. Your parents and siblings have never known anyone else other than this "old you." The more you practice the teachings, the more you will leave old egoistic ways and ideas behind. A "new you" will begin to blossom. Although this will be wonderful to you, if not handled with care, it will be anything but wonderful for your family and friends.

For these people you are changing for the worst. They don't know this "new you." They are attached to the "old you" and will not easily let it go. You will eventually hear some of them tell you that they want the "old you" back. For them your study of the teachings may be likened to a death occurring. The death of the "OLD YOU!" In some ways a death has happened as the "old you" is being moved aside and a new one is coming forth. Why would death of a loved one (you) be a pleasant idea for your family members and friends? Although new and improved versions of things are often desired by people, a "new you" coming forth as a result of your study of the teachings will probably not be a pleasant thing for them. At least initially until they begin to recognize and appreciate the new more considerate virtuous you.

General Considerations on the Impact of Your study of the Teachings on Your Wife/Husband

As you start practicing the teachings, your mate may perceive you as now acting different. Do not be surprised if they start acting as if they think you do not like them. The "new you" will stop drinking and smoking. If your mate was accustomed to drinking and smoking with you, this change could make them feel like you are rejecting them. This may also lead them to feel like you have stopped liking them. If the relationship was having problems at the time you found Shetaut Neter, they may view this "new you" as the writing on the wall for the demise of the relationship. Their view will be correct because the end of the "old you" relationship with them will be ending. Therefore be compassionate with them during this time because they will not have any idea about what is happening. Most importantly, they will not know what to do about it.

Consider that your mate may develop a mindset which sees the relationship as now coming to an end. How many people are able to end any type of relationship without being upset or disappointed? Even people who hate each other are still upset and heartbroken when they break up. This is exactly what is happening in the mind of your mate. Although this relationship breakup does not end with each person physically moving out and moving on, it is a breakup of the internal sort. The internal connection between you and your spouse formed over the years of your relationship is being severed for good. In this context is there any reason for your mate to see this new study of yours as a positive thing for them?

Also keep in mind your mate's perception of your way of being around the house will also change. If you haven't yet, you will soon begin making time for your Sheti practice. You will begin getting up early to pray. You will start doing your yoga postures and will practice meditation. You will find the time to conduct your practice. Your mate will probably not see this as a good thing, especially if you did not have the discipline to do things that would help the relationship. They may even say to you, "Why can you find the time for this yoga stuff and not find the time for me and our relationship?"

To prevent and reduce these types of feelings and situations from occurring, along with making time for your Sheti practice, simultaneously consider making extra time to spend with your mate. Initiate a conversation and let them know that you want to spend more time with them. Set a schedule to spend time with them and honor it without fail. Let them see how your new found discipline not only positively effects you in your personal spiritual practice but also allow them to see how it positively affects them as well. Typically one or two quality moments spent a week with your mate WITHOUT FAIL will alleviate any feelings of discontent from your mate about your new practice. This makes sense since this new time spent with your mate will be more than was occurring before the start of your Sheti practice.

In fact if you do this consistently, over a short period of time, you may quickly find your mate keeping the rest of the family away from you during your Sheti Practice time. At that point they will have a reason to "help" you in your new found practice because they have now begun benefiting from the "new you." They will now have a reason to like the "new you." From their perspective, the practice of the teachings is now changing you for the better. Instead of discouragement, now, you may find them being encouraging to you in your new practice. This will lay a great foundation in your household regarding the teachings. In this environment in their own time, they will begin asking you questions about the teachings. As they see a "new you" that embodies a disciplined loving mate actually living his/her life according to righteousness and virtue, they will not be able to overlook it. Especially since now this "new you" has helped improve your relationship with them.

General Considerations on the impact of YOUR study of the Teachings on YOUR Children

What about your children? How will your new practice impact them? Your children will also see you differently. For example, your practice will strengthen your willpower. Therefore you will develop the willpower to change your eating habits. You will begin to eat meals that are more nutritious. As your eating habits change, you may also force your children to change in this manner as well. Although nutritionally this change is good for them, done abruptly without balance and support from your spouse, this change can create a bad feelings in your children about the teachings.

TV shows that they once watched, you may stop them from seeing. Making them practice the teachings with you when they didn't do anything like this before may be traumatic for them, not because it's anything bad, but because they will see a change in you that they will attribute to the teachings. A change that they will not consider good because the things they are now forced to stop doing are things they consider as good things.

Keep in mind with children that in our teachings, souls before they incarnate choose the circumstances that will best enable them to achieve their own karmic destiny. Therefore, your children have chosen you to be their parents and to be raised in the environment in which they are in. So their souls knew you would eventually be a practitioner of the teachings. This means that whatever you do as you practice the teachings is what they knew they would get before they arrived into time and space. With that in mind consider the following with them. First, become an excellent practitioner of the teachings. Live them and they will see this. This means much more than anything you can make them do. Be an example of the teachings and limit your recitation of them. Next, make sure that whatever change in their daily routine that you want to make, make sure you do this jointly with your spouse. Be careful about arbitrarily changing things on an individual basis. When the decision is made jointly, it will be perceived much differently than if you did it by yourself. When decisions are made independently then the teachings will be considered as the cause. This is not good for anyone.

Finally, let their daily routine stay the same but communicate more about what they do. Engage them in conversation about those things. Let them know that certain beliefs and ideals that they may come into contact with are not in alignment with a way of life that creates joy, peace and complete fulfillment. Explain to them how this happens over and over again if you have to. Eventually they may tire of your talks. They may not. But it is these talks that they may have come to get in the first place by choosing you as one their parents. So be mindful about giving them a reason to have a negative opinion about the teachings. As long as this is done, in due time and season, they will naturally gravitate towards them as this is a reason why they chose you as a parent in the first place.

General Considerations for Dealing with Christian and Muslim Family Members (parents, siblings, friends and co-workers)

It is more likely than not that you will be the only person in your immediate family practicing Shetaut Neter. Although your enthusiasm at the beginning will lead your family members to question you about your new found practice in a light hearted way, this will not last a long time. Right now I am speaking about your extended family members that you see often but do not live with. Your siblings, parents, nephews and nieces etc. Sooner than not, the questions from them will change and the conversation around the family will center on this "cult" like religion you are studying. Keep in mind that both Christianity and Islam are anything but forgiving when it comes to anything outside of their one way to God doctrines. Also keep in mind that for most denominations and sects, their way is the only way. So keep in mind that they will not be listening to you for knowledge about your new found teachings. They will be listening in a way that will allow

"An Aspirant's Guide To Practicing The Egyptian Mysteries"

them the best means to "save" you from this "stuff" you have brought home. Although they may act like they are interested, they really are not. Keep this in mind at all times because the tendency at the beginning will be for you to want to spread the teachings to the people you are the closest to. You will want to share it with them at all times in all places. When they begin to argue or question you, this could be frustrating to you. Especially when you fully realize how ignorant they are based upon their own belief systems. This could also be frustrating because you as a novice student will not be able to fully articulate the teachings.

Be aware that in your personal study of Shetaut Neter, you will come across information about many other religious systems. This **basic** information about other forms of religious practices for students of Shetaut Neter is much more than most religious practitioners know. For many of other religious traditions, for example orthodox Christianity and Islam, practitioners accept wholeheartedly whatever the Bible, Koran, or other spiritual texts say as expressed by the preacher, Imam, or other spiritual teacher. They often have done very little if any study on their own. Therefore their arguments with you will be weak and dogmatic. If you're not careful, these discussions can get out of hand, because you armed with knowledge may make others feel insecure as they have no way of defending their positions with the standard line, "it's God's word and you can't question God."

When you hear this type of statement in the conversation, this is the signal which says that what you have said makes sense but the person you are talking to doesn't want to think about it because it will force them to have to deal with an issue about their faith that they are either not able to do or don't want to do. These types of conversations are sure to happen if you allow them to.

Based on my experience, it is probably best not to mention much of the practice to them at all unless they ask. Speak to only to those who understand you. The best way to express the teachings to them is by living the teachings on a regular basis. There is a saying which says that "actions speak louder than words." As you begin to implement the integrated practice of yoga into your life, the way you live life will change. This will lead to a change in you. Your diet will change. Your patience will change. Your anxiety will lessen. Your anger will subside. You will become calmer. This is the best way to "talk" about the teachings to your extended family members. Do your talking thru your "practice" of the teachings. Trust this. Very few Christians or Muslims actually live their life according to the precepts of their religious doctrine. Many just talk the talk. Your "actions" in living your new found teachings will speak volumes. It will be much louder than any verbal words you may want to say at a family get together or gathering. Your discipline will be the difference. Walking the walk is a much stronger language to convey than just talking about it. If you do this, in a short period of time, your family members will stop trying to "save" you. Most will not stop their Christian or Islamic practice. However, other members of your family not mesmerized by the Christian and Islamic thoughts will see the difference between you and them.

Balance Tips

To further aid the practitioner of the teachings as they interact with family members and friends, the following Balance Tips will assist the aspirant as they begin or intensify their Sheti practices.

As stated previously, the Sheti practices are designed to purify the ego/personality of the person. The implementation of this purification process (the integrated practices of Shetaut Neter) essentially changes your lifestyle. The same is true of your family members and friends. Therefore when implementing the Sheti practices into your daily life, the best results will occur for those people who do these practices with a sense of balance. In this context "practices" is another word for "changes."

The aspirant who actually engages in the daily integrated practices of Shetaut Neter will be changing their entire view of life, what it is and how it is to be lived. As nothing is done in a vacuum, too much change in one area of a person's life, leads to a corresponding change in another area. Therefore, balance as mentioned is necessary when implementing this new lifestyle. But what does balance mean in a person's everyday life and how does it look?

As previously mentioned, your lifestyle change will affect every person in your inner circle. Your spouse, children, family members and friends will feel the effects from this change. Although for example you might think that practice of the "42 Precepts of Maat" in your own life should not be that big of a deal to these people in your life that will not initially be the case with them. To you the cessation of the old habits of lying, stealing, getting jealous and envious is a good thing. For the others, this will mean very little because these habits are not considered as negative by many people. They are considered normal. So it's more likely than not that there won't be a reaction to your newfound virtuous character and nature. If anything, they will initially see you as a bit eccentric and odd.

The following two tips will help you achieve balance as you implement the Sheti spiritual practices into your daily life. The tips are designed specifically to help the reader in dealing with the significant people in his/her life as they begin living their life spiritually.

Balance Tip #1

"Don't tell other people how they should be implementing the 42 precepts (or any other Neterian Practice) in their own lives when you are just beginning to implement them in your own."

Be mindful of preaching the value of your new system of study before you have been seasoned in it. Live according to its precepts and let your life style become the witness to your new study. Most people have never heard of the 42 Precepts of Maat or anything else Neterian. When you inform members of your family about them, don't expect them to suddenly embrace their practice. Even if you tell them that the 10 Commandments come from the Precepts, for many people this will have no effect. There is an old saying which says that "talk is cheap." Talking about the value of the Precepts will mean little to those around you. Living your life according to them will make the most difference.

Balance Tip #2

"Do not be fanatical with the people you associate with regarding your expression to them of the teachings."

It is common for you to want to express to others your excitement for finding the means to your spiritual liberation. But this excitement instead of being a cause for celebration can easily become a cause for heartache and pain.

Why? Because of the way we present the teachings of Shetaut Neter to our inner circle of family and friends. Many times we bring these new found teachings to people from the perspective that this is the end all be all. Therefore, our attitudes can reflect a perception that everybody needs to be studying this. Inherent in this perspective is the belief that every other religious practice is wrong. This mentality is no different from other religious groups who believe that their form of religious practice is the only way. If we are not careful we may make statements like this. "The teachings say we should do this!" "The teachings say we should not do this!" These types of comments create an environment in the household that soon will not be pretty.

For example, as a new practitioner you will begin to watch what you eat and will curtail eating certain types of food altogether. Proper nutrition for the body, mind and spirit will be your key. Be mindful of expressing your new found eating habits from the perspective that the teachings say you should do so. Do not attempt to force your family to immediately alter their eating habits. Forcing them into doing something they do not want to do is fanatical. Presentation of the teachings in this way makes it easy for your mate and family to view the teachings as something negative. This makes sense as you are now "making" them do something that they were not doing before. It will then be easy for them to associate the teachings as being cultish.

It is far more advisable to introduce your mate to eating in a more healthy way by introducing them to articles, columns or books that discuss the benefits of eating in a nutritious way. Then you both can have a dialogue about the pros and cons of implementing a healthy and nutritional diet for your family. Of course you will be eating in a safer way anyway. However, this will not make your mate feel like they are being forced to do anything right away. It will also show them that you respect them and their thoughts. Then although they may not immediately join you in your new found eating style, they will now be able to understand in their own way why you are doing what you are doing. They will then be more prone to be encouraging to you instead of discouraging. Then the only thing that they will be able to say about the teachings is that the teachings have made you health conscious. This is a positive thought good for both you and them. This does not mean that they will immediately become vegetarians. However, this will create the environment which will allow your mate to be receptive to your dietary change and others that will follow.

Conclusion

This is an approach that you can consider when introducing a lifestyle change into the family resulting from the teachings of Shetaut Neter. This is the ultimate form of balance in the practical life setting of the household when approached in this way. Initially, your practice of Shetaut Neter should not make a difference in your home. This will come later. The change in you should be the only difference! Become health conscious. Become conscious of the effects that violence on television and the movies have on you and your family. Become expansive in your conversations about love and religion. Create a dialogue around these topics that makes your family think about them in a way they have not done before. The only change in your household should be the way you think which is now becoming expansive and unlimited. As long as you don't make the members of your family wrong for their views and be a solid practitioner of your new lifestyle, this will say much about Shetaut Neter without words being spoken.

"An Aspirant's Guide To Practicing The Egyptian Mysteries"

"An Aspirant's Guide To Practicing The Egyptian Mysteries"

Smai Tawi

Chapter 4

What Does It Mean to Practice Ancient "Mystical" Spirituality?

Practicing ancient "mystical" spirituality means that you have chosen to live your life in such a way that you spiritualize every part of it. But why do this in the first place? Why engage in a practice that will spiritualize every part of it? Because you have now realized as the Sages, Saints, Priests and Priestesses of days gone by realized, that the soul of the person is heavenly and Divine and that we must "awaken" to this essence which we refer to as the "SELF." You now intellectually understand also that this same essence (SELF) is the underlying essence behind all of creation. However, intellectual understanding at some point must give way to actual "experience." We may state verbally that we are one with the SELF, but until we "know" it thru experience, our words are empty.

The practice of Mystical Spirituality is the means for gaining this experience. Fortunately you also realize that gaining experience of anything requires practice. I can a drive a car once and yes I will now have experience of driving. But it takes many individual driving experiences before I "know" how to drive. Developing experience of our higher nature (SELF) is also an active process requiring self-effort and repeated practice. Just like driving a car requires many experiences before I "know" how to drive, so too does the practice of mystical spirituality require practice. Although the desire to immediately obtain Enlightenment by having an authentic Sage touch our foreheads or shoulders may linger on in our mind, we recognize that spiritual transformation does not work this way. Ancient Egyptian Proverbs on this subject make this clear.

"Salvation is accomplished through the efforts of the individual. There is no mediator between man and his/her salvation."

"Self knowledge is the basis of true knowledge."

"Salvation is the freeing of the soul from its bodily fetters, becoming a God through knowledge and wisdom, controlling the forces of the cosmos instead of being a slave to them, subduing the lower nature and through awakening the Higher Self, ending the cycle of rebirth and dwelling with the Neters who direct and control the Great Plan."

"An Aspirant's Guide To Practicing The Egyptian Mysteries"

"Make your life the subject of intense inquiry, in this way you will discover its goal, direction, and destiny."

"To free the spirit, control the senses; the reward will be clear insight."

"Man is to become God-like through a life of virtue and the cultivation of the spirit through scientific knowledge, practice and bodily discipline."

It is our effort on a daily basis which leads us to the ultimate realization of who we are (SELF). This effort allows us to "know" our heavenly/Divine nature. This makes sense as it was this same effort over many lifetimes which created our present ignorance.

Spiritualizing every daily action means seeing the Divine in every person you speak with. It means feeling the Divine as the wind, rain, or sun when either of them touches you. It means seeing the work that you do as selfless service and purifying works. At its deepest level, it is seeing everything done by you as actually being done by the Divine itself. Most importantly, spiritualizing your life means that you take egoism out of it. This is done through a process called purification.

Purification is a practice which helps a person rid themselves of ideas and beliefs not based in truth. The truth is that we are spiritual beings having an intermittent human experience. Any conscious or unconscious belief contrary to this truth prevents a person from achieving spiritual emancipation. The purification process clears the conscious and unconscious aspects of mind of thoughts contrary to this. These thoughts are reflected through the ego of a person.

The ego of a person is an idea of who they think they are. It is not real in a substantive sense as you cannot feel or touch it. All people have one. The difference between people is whether they have a purified or unpurified ego. Enlightened sages and those with elevated personalities have a purified ego. The ego of an enlightened person does not obstruct the experience of oneness with the Self, so enlightened Sages experience expansion. He or she experiences the underlying common reality behind all things in Creation. It gravitates towards identifying with the similarities between objects and things. Inner peace, joy, contentment and happiness are common in people with purified egos.

A person with an unpurified ego sees him/ herself as an individual entity in the midst of other individual entities. He/she sees their self as a limited human being at the mercy of life and its processes. They identify with differences between others and things. Anger, frustration, envy, and jealousy to name a few are found in people with unpurified egos.

The purification process is what allows spiritual awakening to occur. Life lived in this way allows the "mystical" aspect of the practice to have its intended effect. This is what it means to practice the "mystical" aspect of religion.

Sheta (Mystery), Sheta (Hidden)

Chapter 5

What Is Shetaut Neter And Its Purpose?

Shetaut Neter can be defined as the "study of the secret, hidden mysterious nature of the Divine or God." Shetaut means secret, hidden and/or mysterious. Neter means Divine or God in the singular sense. Neter in this context refers to the One God from which all things come into being. This is what the term Shetaut Neter means.

The "Kemetic Tree of Life" book by Dr. Muata Ashby on page 27 defines Shetaut Neter in the following way. "Shetaut Neter as a term comes from Ancient Kamit/Egypt. These Black African people created a vast civilization and culture earlier than any other society in known history. They also organized a nation that was based upon the concepts of balance and order (Maat) as a foundation for the practice of religion and the pursuit of spiritual enlightenment (Nehast). The spiritual leaders of Kamit, the priests and priestesses, realized that there was a deeper aspect of human existence and higher dimensions of reality. They also realized that there was an intelligent underlying transcendental consciousness that was/is the essence of Creation. They then developed spiritual systems that were designed to allow human beings to understand the nature of this secret being that is the essence of all Creation. They called this system Shetaut Neter.

Purpose of the Shetaut Neter Practice

The purpose of the Shetaut Neter practice is to provide you with the tools that will allow you to have the type of life you say that you want, a life filled with freedom, joy, and peace in this lifetime. In our tradition the highest expression of this life is embodied in the term called Nehast/Enlightenment.

A practice is something that a person does on a regular basis. This regular practice makes them proficient in that area. There are two types of practices. One is conscious and the other is unconscious. Any practice done with the goal of improving something is a conscious practice of that thing. Going to the driving range to improve a golf swing is a conscious practice. An unconscious practice occurs anytime a person engages in an activity on a regular basis without a goal of becoming better at it. Driving a car is an example of an unconscious practice.

Therefore the regular conscious or unconscious engagement of an activity is a practice of that activity. Although not all agree that practice makes perfect, many agree that practice makes permanent. Those that consciously practice an activity know what their desired outcome is. Those that engage in unconscious practices do not realize the process that is occurring.

The African Kamitic Sages and Saints realized that there was an aspect of life that many people are not aware of. They realized that there is a plane beyond the mind and senses which give rise to Creation as we know it. This plane exists beyond time and space. They realized that this plane could only be realized by a person free from the belief that the full extent of reality can be perceived through the five senses. The more they dwelled in this plane the more they realized that life as most people know it is only a reflection of that which is true at all times. They then developed a series of "practices" which if followed would lead other people to this same "realization." This realization is known in our tradition as Nehast/Enlightenment.

Nehast is the term used to describe the highest level of spiritual awakening. It means attaining such a level of spiritual awareness that one discovers the underlying unity of the entire universe as well as the fact that the source of all creation is the same source from the Self within which every human heart arises.[1] Its manifestation can be seen in those who experience abiding peace and happiness which is unaffected by any worldly occurrence.

The "realization" for all people of different backgrounds and faiths are the same. However, in other cultures and religious traditions, the terms used to describe this "realization" differ. Resurrection, Nehast, Salvation, The Kingdom of Heaven, Moksha or Liberation, Buddha Consciousness, One with the Tao, Self-Realization, Know Thyself, etc. The purpose of the Shetaut Neter practices is to achieve this state (awareness) in this lifetime.

---

[1] The Egyptian Book of the Dead, by Dr. Muata Ashby.

SECTION II

Common Obstacles while engaged In the Daily Practice of Shetaut Neter

Each chapter in this section deals with a specific obstacle that I have experienced as I have practiced the "Mysteries." You may or may not experience them. However, they will help give you an overview of the way life plays itself out once the teachings are practiced on a daily basis. As stated previously, at the beginning of my practice of the teachings I had a glorified idea about what being a student of teachings meant.

Although I was told and understood through reading all of the books that spiritual liberation occurs incrementally, deep down inside, I still wanted to believe that my life would suddenly change for the better. I even thought that all my problems would immediately go away. For some this might be the case. For me it was not. It is my desire that those who read the chapters in this section and apply what they find to their own life will allow their practice to be as smooth and quick as possible.

"An Aspirant's Guide To Practicing The Egyptian Mysteries"

NEBERDJER

The All Encompassing Divinity

Chapter 6

Belief in Gender
A Big Obstacle to Spiritual Growth and Development

"Souls, Heru, son, are of the self-same nature in themselves, nor male nor female are they. Sex is a thing of bodies, not of souls."

-Teachings of Aset to Heru

As a student and practitioner of the mystical teachings of Shetaut Neter, I have found that there are obstacles which must be overcome to grow spiritually. There are a few which will be discussed in later chapters but the one presented now is to me by far the most difficult one to deal with. The belief in gender has been the biggest obstacle to me for one main reason. It is so subtle that it is easy to not even recognize it. This occurs because in modern society it is unconsciously "understood" that differences in gender are inherently "real." The following example will illustrate what I mean by this, and how recognition of this obstacle was difficult for me.

There was a cartoon children's movie out a few years ago named "The Lion King." In the movie, the lead character was a lion cub whose father was the King of the jungle. The character's name was Simba. Therefore Simba the lion cub was the heir to the throne. However, the cub's uncle was evil and had his own ambitions. He wanted to be king and would stop at nothing to become so. The uncle plotted against his brother, Simba's father, and had him killed. In the process, he tricked Simba into believing that his father's death was his fault. Resultantly Simba ran away and the evil uncle assumed the throne.

The Lion King story is a replica of the epic African Kamitic story called the Asarian Resurrection. Hamlet, Star Wars and its central character Luke Skywalker, and also the story of Krishna in India are replicas of the Asarian Resurrection also. These stories while entertaining do much more than entertain. They impart spiritual wisdom about the nature of the soul of every person and how that soul can discover its true essence as one with the Divine.

"An Aspirant's Guide To Practicing The Egyptian Mysteries"

Simba was very young when he ran away. Therefore he did not know what it meant to be a lion. In fact he was so young when all of this happened that he didn't really know what a lion was. Before his father was murdered, he had not yet really gotten to know him and had not yet been taught in the ways, customs and traditions of his family. In short he did not know who he was. On top of this, he did not know that he did not know who he was.

While in the other areas of the jungle, he befriended two other animals. One I recall being a warthog and the other a meerkat. As he grew up around them he emulated the ways and customs of both. Although he did an admiral job under the circumstances of acting like both a warthog and meerkat, frustration and discontent was his state of being for the majority of his time. Simply put, a lion cannot be anything other than a lion no matter how much he tried not to be. This was the cause of his frustration although as a cub and young lion he was not aware/conscious of this. Anytime something or someone attempts to be something other than what they actually are, frustration and discontent will always be present even if they do not consciously realize it.

Personally I can recall that ever since I was a small child I inherently understood that I was a "boy." For those of you with female energy forms, you probably can relate to the fact that you inherently understood that you were always a "girl." No one that I remember ever told me point blank that I was a male child or boy. No one ever told me point blank as I grew older that I was becoming a man. The closest way in which this was ever expressed to me was in statements that talked about how boys do this or that boys don't do that. But I don't recall anyone directly telling me about what my gender was. However, I have understood from the earliest times in my life that I was a "male."

Like the young lion cub from the movie, I too grew up attempting to be something that I was not. Ultimately we know from philosophy to science that all that exists in creation are nothing more than what appears to be individuated manifestations of "One" underlying essence. This "essence" is known by different names in different traditions but the "essence" is the same thing.

If I choose to categorize myself, the best method of doing so is to call myself a "male energy form" and not a male person. This is because everything at its base is nothing more than energy vibrating at different rates of speed. The different vibratory states are what give rise to the appearance of differences in things. Although the distinction between being a "male energy form" and a male person may seem slight, upon reflection and review, it is not. This is because it is this distinction which creates what I consider to be the biggest obstacle to achieving spiritual liberation. This obstacle is the belief that inherently we are our gender.

Keep in mind the following about Simba the lion cub. While he was in the jungle away from home, he had no way of knowing who he was. Home represents the place or mindset needed that allows a person to know who they are so they can be who they are. Because he was away from home, (away from the knowledge of who he was) he mistakenly identified himself with what his friends were. Consequently he ate like them. He played like them and most importantly, he thought like them. With every action he took like them, he reinforced a mistaken notion about who he was. For Simba, it took a significant event in his life to figure out that he was actually something altogether different from what he had grown up mistakenly believing.

It is important to recognize that the event giving rise to "realization" for Simba did not automatically confer enlightened consciousness upon him. After living most of his life acting outside of his natural lion nature, when he finally "realized" who he really was, initially, he found it difficult to act like a lion.

I too grew up not knowing who I was. I too grew up believing that I was something that I was not. In my case I grew up believing that I was a male child and everything I did from being a toddler to an adult did nothing but reinforce this mistaken belief. I too ate like other males and people. I too played with other males and people in the way that they do. I too engaged in the rituals of partying and mating like other males and so called human beings do. With every act, I reinforced the mistaken notion that I was a limited male human being. I had no clue that I was actually a male energy form.

This is important to keep in mind. Although Simba was in actuality a lion and heir to the throne, he did not "know" it. He believed something else. Therefore instead of living into his greatness, he lived into the limited notions that he identified with from what he saw around him.

I too identified with limited notions of who I was. I too believed that I was something I was not. I was not and am not a limited male human being. I am an energetic essence that is One with all that there is that transcends physicality and time and space. When you think about it like this, it is actually quite awesome. However, how can I live into that when I mistakenly believe that I am a human with approximately 75 years on Earth to live before I can die and then hopefully be happy if I make it to heaven?

This is why gender is a very difficult obstacle standing in the way of spiritual liberation. The belief that we are male or female is "understood" by a large number of people. This notion is also reinforced by the culture that is in place presently as well. This makes this a "subtle belief" that few even realize they have. Simply put what is there to "know" when something else is allegedly "understood?"

Spiritual liberation cannot occur until a person is ready to let go of their notions that they are a specific gender even while continuing to act as a certain gender in practical life. As energy is genderless, identification with the underlying essence of who we are will not happen until we let go of our notions of gender.

On its face, the mistaken notion of who a person inherently is can be dealt with rather easily. Come into the knowledge of who you are really and then live in accordance with that knowledge. This is what eventually happened in the Lion King movie.

But easy on its face is not so easy when we come to grips with the impact that our actions in the world have on our unconscious mental notions of who we are. At the deepest level of our being, we have come to believe that we are something we are not. In my case I believed that I was a male. This belief that I am a male "caused" me to engage in actions which were male- like. Each action left an "impression/ari" in this innermost deep region of my being. The more I engaged in these actions, the more "ari" that was deposited. The more "ari" that was deposited, the easier it became to continue acting male like the other males did. Conversely these same actions made it difficult for me to be able to "accept" the knowledge of who I was/am.

Although at a certain point I did come into this knowledge, this information did not immediately transform me. In fact, in some ways this knowledge made my life appear to be quite more difficult. This is because this knowledge was a 360 degree contradiction of what I had grown up not even questioning. It was also because at the moment of coming into this knowledge, I was still acting in accordance with that of other males in society. So although I was mentally beginning to accept the premise of my divine nature, I was still acting in a degraded

"An Aspirant's Guide To Practicing The Egyptian Mysteries"

way based upon the sense pleasure pursuits of in my case other males. This is why I believe many who find the path are not always immediately able to live the path as they do not realize the upheaval going on in the unconscious aspect of our being. (When two things are being dealt with instead of one. Mistaken notion of being male vs. actual reality of my divine nature)

Think about it. How can I really be "one with the Divine" and believe that all I see, touch, taste, hear and smell is all One, when I am still chasing that woman, or car, or home or money that still seems to provide pleasure to me? My chase itself is a movement based upon identification with those things as being separate and distinct from myself. So a dual movement takes place as I intellectually "think" like I am a part of the whole while I simultaneously "act" like I am an individual among other individuals. Do not be surprised that while on the path, this type of convergence will take place in your life also. This is an example of how the two aspects of every person, Heru and Set, are at war with each other until Nehast dawns.

However, do not consider this as something bad or negative. It is something to watch and prepare for, nothing more and nothing less. This is why the integrated practice of yoga is enjoined so that this convergence will not be so rocky. No matter what you may see and what you have been led to believe, you are not a male. No matter what you have heard and what you thought, you are not a female. You are energy in the form of a male or female to receive lessons needed for your spiritual liberation. This aspect is infinite and eternal. It is this aspect that you really are. However this aspect is genderless. It cannot be found for the person who believes that they are a gender. For this person the Akhu will remain a mystery.

To be clear I do not mean to suggest that the problem is the male or female gender. Rather the problem is the identification in my case as my male body being the essence of who I am. I am not suggesting that I must act in a gender neutral way to attain Nehast. Rather you must acknowledge that even though you might be expressing as a male or female personality, your true Soul essence is without gender.

As an initiate, your goal is to become aware of this higher aspect of your being. The sooner it is realized that we exist beyond gender, the sooner this goal will be achieved. Again like Aset said to Heru,

"Souls, Heru, son, are of the self-same nature in themselves, nor male nor female are they. Sex is a thing of bodies, not of souls."

Vignette of the Rising Sun-Papyrus Kenna

Chapter 7

Something to Consider,
Ideas Shape Reality!

When beginning a spiritual practice, deep reflection should be given too many areas of your life. A concerted effort should be made to become aware of the ideas that you presently have which form the basis of what you believe life is and its purpose. An unconscious process occurs in many people that influences this view. Quite often people allow what was originally an idea to change into a belief. Instead of having ideas to be considered, beliefs form the basis of how we view and live life. This is unfortunate for a couple of reasons. First the process is unconscious. It is practically impossible to deal with something when we are oblivious to it. Second, living life based upon a large number of beliefs instead of ideas, makes it easy to stop the evolutionary process of life. Living life based upon what is now "believed" to be true makes it difficult to fully evolve as a human being. Simply put, a person stops him/herself from growing and evolving when their reality of life is based upon beliefs instead of ideas.

As soon as a mind changes from the "idea" mode to the "belief" mode a shift in consciousness takes place. The shift immediately renders the mind as fixed, rigid and inflexible. A mind that "believes" something is a mind now that can no longer be changed. The "belief" becomes not only a fact but also a reality. A person who "believes" something is not accepting of new information about that thing. At the heart of a "belief" is a thought without any fact or experience to support it. In spite of this lack of support, people conceptualize their beliefs and act on them as if they are actually facts. This is unfortunate because of what happens when new information is brought to a mind that has a "belief." No matter how relevant or true, information which contradicts a "belief" is immediately disregarded by the mind. This process keeps this person stuck in a pattern in which they grow and evolve physically but mentally their minds do not.

Unfortunately many are not aware that this process is occurring. An idea which changes into a belief is also damaging in another way. It colors our view of what the world is and how we should function in it.

At their root, most ideas/realities are premised on people being limited mortal human beings with no connection to the Divine.

Most importantly this reality "drives" our new thoughts and thought processes. In short, this new "belief/reality" causes us to have new thoughts which reinforce and support the mistaken "belief/reality." This creates a never ending unconscious cycle and renders the mind dull.

A life lived with the awareness of this normally unconscious process allows a person to be in TOTAL control of every aspect of their life. This person can grow and evolve because he/she does not allow his/her mind to become rigid and inflexible. As his/her physical body grows and evolves, so too does his/her mind since he/she is easily able to integrate new knowledge and experiences into his/her way of thinking about the world. This person is in charge of his/her life because he/she does not allow him/herself to become victims of his/her mind. Such people control their minds by allowing them to be flexible. They keep themselves in the position in which they are conscious about what they adopt as "real" and what they see as "illusionary."

This awareness allows them to change easily when change is warranted. It is easy to change an idea. Acquire new information which resonates with you and instantly you can change your mind which simultaneously changes behavior. This is what it means to grow and evolve, to learn new information or learn new things from experiences. Then, consciously integrate these new things into your personality and you have an evolving personality type.

The inability to recognize the areas in your life where you now have beliefs instead of ideas will slow your spiritual movement. Because the process is unconscious, the underlying "beliefs" in the typical mind of a person is likely to reflect the common view of society. Namely, that we are limited human beings, separate and individual with no connection to the Divine. The more "beliefs" a person has that are centered in this way, the more impressions/ari that are stored in the unconscious part of their mind. Impressions/ari can be likened to the Indian term Karma in that "you reap what you sow." However the Kamitic term "Ari" explains exactly how this process happens.

Ari
"Action," "to do something," "things done"
(From Chapter 33 of the *Prt m Hru*)

Every action/thought contains a certain amount of energy. So when a person has a thought to do something, a certain amount of energy is behind the thought. This energy leaves an impression in the unconscious mind. This is true whether the thought is positive or negative. As this person has the same thought over and over again, more energy is built up. Over time the person will be compelled by the force of the built up energy to "act" out on the impression. For example, if a person is told by their doctor that they should not eat chocolate cake, they may develop the idea/impression that they are missing out on something. This idea/impression like all others carries with it a certain amount of energy. Every time this person is reminded about not eating chocolate cake, they again think that they are missing out on something. Each reminder contains energy and this energy builds up on top of the energy buildup from earlier.

It is easy to see that it will be a short matter of time before this person will be compelled to eat some chocolate cake. Although their mind will remind them about what the doctor said, the energy built up about missing out on something they consider as good, will compel them to act otherwise.

Unawareness of this process places a person at the mercy of this energy. This is the reason why people really do not have choices when faced with the myriad number of decisions faced in everyday life. What is referred to as acting on impulse is nothing more than being compelled to act based upon the buildup of energy stored from previous impressions.

Ultimately there are only two assumptions underlying the ideas/beliefs a person has about every area of their life.

A) That you are a limited human being separate and apart from the Divine/God; or
B) That you are an aspect of the whole which is the Divine beyond name and form unlimited in breadth and scope. (Neteru)

What follows in the next section are areas of life where ideas easily turn into beliefs. Consideration of the underlying assumption in each area is something you may benefit from if you do it. As you look at the numbered areas, ask yourself the following questions about each one.

1. What is the current idea that I have in this area?

2. Where did the idea come from?
3. Did I make a conscious choice to adopt this idea or was it an unconscious one?
4. Is the idea true?
5. Will the idea stand the test of time?[2]
6. Has the idea now become a belief?

If you did not make a conscious choice to adopt a particular way of life, then it is more likely than not that you now have a "belief" in that area instead of an idea. A "belief" which probably supports the assumption that you are a limited, mortal, human being, separated and apart from everything.

To facilitate a clear understanding of how this process works consider the following example based upon my own past experience. The area I will analyze is **Love in Male-Female Relationships**. The answers that follow are based upon application of my own past personal experience.

1. ***What is the current idea I have in this area?*** The current idea I have in this area is that I know a woman loves me when she satisfies the majority of my wants and needs. Satisfaction by her in this way means that she loves me. When she stops satisfying my wants and needs in this way, this means that her love for me has stopped.

2. ***Where did the idea come from?*** I don't know where the idea came from. It's something I know and have always known.

3. ***Did I make a conscious choice to adopt this idea or was it an unconscious one?*** I never gave thought to this idea or its adoption. In fact I never even imagined that this was something I should even think about. Love as manifested like this is the only way about love that I have ever known. That's all I knew, therefore, my adoption of this idea must have been an unconscious one.

4. ***Is the idea true?*** For most of my life this idea about love in male-female relationships seemed true as this was all I knew. But today I'm not so sure. It seems like there are more people miserable in relationships than happy. This idea does not seem to be true.

---

[2] From the book "You Are Responsible For Your Life!" by Lawrence R. Mathews

5. **Will the idea stand the test of time?** The idea that love is manifested in a relationship when a mate is satisfying wants and needs will not last. The idea does not work right now so it does not seem plausible that it can stand the test of time. This idea will be lucky to last another twenty years.

Given the fact that I did not consciously choose this idea about love in my relationships, I easily moved from the "idea" stage to the "belief" stage without realizing it. This is also known as conditioning. Therefore, I needed help to realize what I was doing. I got this help from the integrated practice of Yoga. The process of purifying the ego helped me "see" how this was happening.

A life lived operating from many beliefs instead of ideas impedes the spiritual movement because it reinforces the unconscious belief that we are limited human beings. Beliefs give credence to the so called fact that reality is composed only of that which we perceive with our senses and conditioned minds. However, our core essence is striving to "remember" itself as one with the universe and the Divine.

An important function of an authentic teaching is the cleansing of the unconscious aspect of our being from the belief that we are limited human beings. By now you are aware at least intellectually that you are in fact the Self, The Divine, God.

Therefore, there is nothing we really have to do but remember this. The problem is that we have forgotten this aspect of ourselves. The spiritual practice allows us to cleanse ourselves of thoughts and impressions which "veil" our ability to realize this.
To assist in this cleansing process, consider making a category list of different aspects of your life. Then for each one, answer the questions as given previously. Here is a sample of a few areas.

1. Happiness;
2. sadness;
3. forgiveness;
4. love;
5. anger;
6. contentment;
7. religion;
8. success;
9. failure;

10. responsibility;
11. fear;
12. excitement;
13. beauty;
14. truth;
15. fiction;
16. race;
17. nutrition;
18. reality;
19. spirituality;
20. sex life;
21. prejudice;
22. death;
23. life;
24. family;
25. life on other planets;
26. soul;
27. god;
28. heaven;
29. hell;
30. Intimacy.

These are just a few to get you started. There are many more. All of the ideas that you have about these areas of your life and others form the basis of who you "believe" yourself to be. In fact, these previous "ideas" now turned into "beliefs" constitute the "reality" of the world you live in and experience. For those who can say that every area of their life is based upon the underlying assumption that we are unlimited expressions of the Divine connected to all at all times, their spiritual movement will be quick. Those with the opposite view will find their spiritual movement slowed as they have to cleanse their minds of this illusion.

Do not think that as a Yoga practitioner of Shetaut Neter that you will not have a period in which you will have a belief system phase. Everything mentioned about the underlying essence that gives rise to and supports all of creation is only a belief until it is experienced. In this case belief is a means to an end and necessary until you acquire mystical insight and experiences of this essence. Here the idea about beliefs differs greatly from those in main stream society.

The common denominator about ideas without the underlying basis that the Divine is the subtle essence making up all things is that they will not stand the test of time. It may take one hundred years, or it may only take a year or months, but eventually ideas change as people continue growing, evolving, and learning more about life and the world around them.

Do you allow your ideas to change as you change? Will your ideas about the topics expressed previously stand the test of time? Or will future generations find today's idea about their practice to be archaic and backwards? If your present ideas on these topics will not stand the test of time, should you base your outlook on life on an idea that is not true?

Living your life-making decisions and acting in certain ways that are based on believing an idea that is untrue means that you are living your life based on an illusion.

Forms of the God Djehuti

"An Aspirant's Guide To Practicing The Egyptian Mysteries"

Chapter 8

The Relationship between the Spiritual Preceptor and the World

A major obstacle to practicing the teachings effectively is the fact that people tend to make things personal. When life's challenges present themselves, we often believe that we are the only people experiencing a negative circumstance. This idea makes it easy for us to believe that we are unlucky or that there is something wrong with us. In the extreme case, we may even blame God for our circumstance. While it is true that present circumstances are a result of previous actions, what is not always realized is the purpose behind having the present circumstance in the first place. If properly understood, all life challenges are lessons from the world which moves a person closer to the realization of Nehast.

The Spiritual Preceptor is a Sage and Wisdom teacher. He/She imparts the teachings which provide guidance to the aspirant on their spiritual quest. Therefore, the Preceptor and the world function in a similar capacity, helping guide one to Nehast. The major difference between the two is the time frame needed to achieve this state from each. Lessons from the world occur over several lifetimes thru the process of reincarnation/Meskenet. In fact, it could take over one thousand lifetimes to reach this state this way. The use of an authentic teaching with a Spiritual Preceptor shortens the time immensely. Nehast can be achieved with an authentic teaching and authentic teacher in this present lifetime.

As students of the teachings we do not always realize that we have chosen to combine the two. We receive lessons from both the Preceptor and the World. Thru the guidance of the Preceptor and the experiences from the world, we get the opportunity to practice our understanding of the teachings in actual circumstances. This practice allows the aspirant to steadily, mentally transcend their ideas about the "reality" of the world. The more a person mentally transcends circumstances commonly experienced in the world, the more he/she transcends their limited understanding of what the world is completely.

As a person encounters life's ups and downs while practicing the teachings, a couple of points may help in not making life situations personal. First, no experience is going to last forever. As surely as experiences will come, they will also go. Second, life's ups and downs are individuated lessons designed specifically for each person to overcome. They do not occur as punishments. They occur to be conquered. Spiritual realization grows as each circumstance is overcome. Therefore, there is nothing wrong with so called negative situations in the world. In fact, they are Divine messengers which if handled properly, allow a person to grow spiritually.

Time

As life challenges present themselves, keep in mind the illusory nature of time. Often while in the midst of a troubling situation, it seems like the ordeal lasts for long periods of time. Sometimes it seems like the situation is never going to end. This can breed frustration and anxiety, which makes the time appear to last for even longer periods. The belief that difficult moments are never going to end is erroneous, and makes it tough to practice spirituality. What appears to be a long time period is in fact anything but long. In actuality it is very short.

It only appears to be long because of our attachment to the idea that the circumstance is real. The deeper the attachment to the so-called reality of the circumstance, the longer the circumstance appears to last. However, this is not the truth. What is occurring happens over a very short span of time. The time frame is more akin to a blink of an eye. The following segment from the ancient Egyptian "Instruction to Mer-Ka-Re'" explains this from a philosophical point of view.

"You know that they are not merciful the day when they judge the miserable one...Do not count on the passage of the years; they consider a lifetime as but an hour. After death man remains in existence and his acts accumulate beside him. Life in the other world is eternal, but he who arrives without sin before the Judge of the Dead, he will be there as a Neter and he will walk freely as do the masters of eternity." (Emphasis added)

The reference above to "they consider lifetime as but an hour" alludes to the aspect of time in the higher realms. If reflected and meditated on, this understanding of time can assist the aspirant when dealing with the daily challenges of life. If an entire lifetime is actually occurring over a span of an hour, what does that say about a life situation that lasts for 20 years? Wouldn't that be actual time of approximately twenty minutes? What about a life situation that lasts for two or three years? That would be approximately five minutes right? What about life circumstances that occur over a span of months? That would be seconds of actual time would it not?

Consider the following. No matter your present age, you can recall with vivid memory being a young child, teenager and young adult. Many say that "it seems like yesterday" when they were children. When this moment happens, the reality of the time construct can clearly be seen. TIME FLIES! Without attachment to the belief in the reality of the situation, time occurs at a rapid pace.[3]

Ultimately all circumstances quickly come and go. Understanding this concept of time in the midst of life's challenges will assist you in quickly detaching from the so-called reality of the situation.

Life's Challenges are Individuated Opportunities to Grow Spiritually

As you receive guidance from the Preceptor and experiences thru the world, understanding the "nature" of what we call life's challenges helps us understand and better handle them. One consistent fact about life is that things are always changing. Nothing stays the same. Life is marked by transiency. Therefore, expecting for things today to be as they were yesterday is an idea not based upon a basic fact of life. Often what appears as a challenge of life is nothing more than an attachment to an idea of how things "used" to be. Therefore the expectation is that those same things "should" be the same as they were previously. I can only have an employment life challenge as long as I believe I am supposed to have a job. I can only have a relationship challenge as long as I believe I am supposed to have a mate who acts a particular way.

Looking at these "ideas" in this way does not mean that I should not work, nor does it mean that I should abstain from dating. What it does mean is that my "idea" of what having a job or a relationship means to me is actually the cause of the so-called challenging circumstance. Detachment is the term used to describe the process of clearing the mind of these types of ideas which are not based in truth.

The Preceptor provides detailed instruction concerning the doctrine of detachment. Instruction is also provided to let the aspirant know that *"searching for happiness in the world of time and space is the search for an illusion."* This is an Ancient Egyptian Proverb. Although this instruction is provided, aspirants are not always immediately able to apply this to their daily life.

---

[3] For purposes of this Chapter, the description of "time" is given for ease of reference. Ultimately time like space are constructs of the mind and do not exist in any "real" sense.

It is at this time that the world provides a playground if you will of on the job training in this way. Thru our previous actions, the world provides us with situations which allow us to practice the instruction provided.

The world is not against anyone. Its job is to give those in it a realm to develop spiritually in an expeditious way. This is done thru presenting a person with experiences that force them to deal with their underlying erroneous ideas about that circumstance. Aspirants who choose to deal with this thru the instruction provided by the Preceptor and/or Teaching are engaged in the practice of detachment. Those that choose otherwise are engaged in the cycle of birth-death-rebirth (uhem ankh reincarnation/Meskenet).

Ultimately, "life challenges" do not exist. Life is nothing more than a series of events designed to lead a person to Self-Knowledge. Circumstances within life become challenging when we allow "ideas" about our lives which are not in accordance with the truth, to reign supreme.

"An Aspirant's Guide To Practicing The Egyptian Mysteries"

ANPU

Discernment and Discriminative Knowledge of What is Real and What is Not Real.

THE GODS OF THE SENSES

Above-Relief showing the gods of the senses (from the Temple of Heru at Ed

Chapter 9

What You See Is What You Get!

A group known as "The Dramatics," made a song in the mid 70's called "What You See, Is What You Get!" It is the perfect title for this chapter as it expresses a thought, which if not handled properly, can hinder your practice on the spiritual path.

A big obstacle that you may encounter as you practice the teachings is fully accepting the impact that in this world, what you "see" regularly is ALL that you or anyone can "get" regularly. Although for most of my life I held onto the belief that I was somehow "different" from all others, I now know this to be anything but true. I used to believe that the obtainment of "some thing" was the cure all for life's maladies. No matter how often I "saw" others who had secured this "thing" miserable and unhappy, I thought that somehow I was/am different from them. Although I "saw" that what they had did not "get" them what I or they deem to be important, unconditional happiness, complete joy, fulfillment and peace, I unconsciously chose to ignore what was staring me in the face.

One of the obstacles I faced as I began and continued my practice of the teachings was my reluctance to accept that what I saw in the world on a daily basis was/is all that the world has to offer. Therefore, no matter how much I overlooked it in my past and on occasion still may want to overlook it today, what I see in the world is all I can get from the world. Although I may hope that there is a light at the end of the tunnel of the world, there is not one. You, like me, may not initially want to deal with this fact. You, like me, may temporarily choose to ignore it. However the fact of the matter is that the world can provide you with nothing more than it is giving you right now. A Kamitic Proverb about this tells us why this is so.

"Searching for one's self in the world is the pursuit of an illusion."

Although I have struggled over the years with the belief that there is some ultimate abiding happiness, peace and contentment to be found in the worldly way of living and practicing life, the full realization that "what you see is what you get" came to a head for me today.

"An Aspirant's Guide To Practicing The Egyptian Mysteries"

It began when I completed seeing Tyler Perry's movie called "Why Did I Get Married Too?" Watching it was interesting to say the least. At its conclusion, I remember remarking to my girlfriend at the time that, "if an alien space creature who knew nothing about relationships was to view this movie, they could easily say that there is no point to being involved in one at all." Each couple in the movie had serious issues and none of them were able to deal with them in a less than dysfunctional way. Objectively speaking, there was no redeeming quality to be found in any of the couples. But for the fact that each couple as depicted in the movie acted in a common degraded way, nothing I saw provided a basis for desiring a relationship of any of these kinds.

And that is what brought this to a head for me. This is what is the most interesting, that these types of relationships are COMMON! They are nothing out of the ordinary! They are "NORMAL" in general western societal cultures! Although in my past and recent present I have been reluctant to accept this, in this current societal way of thinking, what you "see" in relationships as depicted in the movie is exactly what you will most likely "get" when involved in one. You may get something less. Most importantly, you don't get anything "more".

This is because the masses of people in western culture do not follow mystical spirituality traditions such as Shetaut Neter. Therefore, they believe themselves to be individuals and that true happiness is something that can be acquired externally thru relationships as an example. But because true abiding happiness can only be achieved by becoming Enlightened, people in relationships hold unrealistic expectations of the other person- that the other person for example does in fact make them happy, and consequently, is also the reason they are unhappy. Typical western societal cultural thinking for most is that it's the other person's duty to make you happy. When the partners in the relationship fail to make each other happy, even for a short time, much less than abidingly, they start fighting and blaming each other. They may even cheat on the other person thinking that the problem is their partner so they only need to get with another person. Surely the problem was that they picked the wrong person initially. So people go from relationship to relationship doing the same thing over and over again while expecting to get a different result.

The "more" part is what is important to focus on when engaged in a spiritual practice. "More" is the belief that MY relationship will somehow be "different" from the others. Unfortunately it took me awhile to realize that there is no basis for this thought. Why would my relationship differ from others? What makes mine different? Have I been around others whose relationships have been different to model? Or are all those worldly relationships that I have been exposed to the same? Have I COMPLETELY eliminated my own thoughts about sense pleasure and desire seeking being the basis for how I live life? If I haven't looked at all of these things, what basis do I have to believe that I will have "more" in the relationship setting than what I see?

The "more" part also does one other thing on the spiritual path. It creates a veil over our ability to see things as they are. As long as I choose to believe that things can be "more" than what they presently are, I can continue to seek out relationships for the purpose of sense pleasure and desire satisfaction, all without realizing that sense pleasure and desire satisfaction is really what I am chasing. Ultimately this is what hinders the spiritual practice, the unconscious attachment to a continued seeking out of activities that will satisfy the desire of sense pleasures and pleasure seeking."

This would be bad enough if this only happened in the world of male-female relationships. But acceptance of things as they are is not limited to male/female relationships only. In the areas of recreation, play, and leisure, "what you see is what you get" is also ignored. Drinking is considered to be a pleasurable experience even though alcohol destroys blood cells. For many, drinking until one becomes sick is pleasurable. Despite the fact that many people are killed because of drunk drivers, drinking somehow is still considered to be fun in general western societal ways of thinking. Obviously "what you see is what you get," is ignored in this context.

Smoking cigarettes and the use of other drugs damage the body and its cellular structure. Although we "see" people die due to the effects of smoking every day, we think we will "get" a different result because we are somehow different. Again "what you see is what you get" is ignored. Even the so-called relaxing night out to listen to soft music or to go to a concert or comedy show ultimately does nothing but provide a means of escapism from the problems that living in the world according to its ideas about what life is creates.

But escapism does nothing to help solve the problems one is attempting to escape from in the first place. Although one might get a break for an hour or two, the problem remains. Eventually it will still have to be dealt with. And this is what is so tragic. Instead of looking at the underlying cause of the situation the person is attempting to escape from, we again lead ourselves to believe that we are somehow different from all others.

Unfortunately "what you see is what you get," does little to help a person realize and face a major issue in their life. Not knowing that the true source of happiness in life is the Higher Self! Lack of this knowledge causes people to seek happiness through relationships. It is also the cause behind feelings of incompleteness and a sense of inadequacy.

For the spiritual practitioner who wants to pierce thru, uncover, and experience what is "mysterious" to most people, the Divine, FULL ACCEPTANCE of "what you see is what you get" is important. Until this happens, the practitioner is doing nothing more than giving him/herself an unconscious reason to seek out sense pleasure seeking and desire satisfaction. As long as we allow ourselves to believe that things for us can be more than what they appear, then what we are saying is the following: "I still want to satisfy my desires, passions, and sense pleasures!" Needless to say this hinders spiritual evolution in a tremendous way.

"What you see in the world, is all you get from the world" is a profound spiritual realization. What you "see" is the BEST that this culture has to offer not what you hope for. Once it is realized that this best is not what we make it out to be, the destination to Nehast gets much shorter.

"An Aspirant's Guide To Practicing The Egyptian Mysteries"

NEBERDJER

The All Encompassing Divinity

"An Aspirant's Guide To Practicing The Egyptian Mysteries"

NEBETHET

"Mistress of the House"

Nature, Worldly Consciousness and Death

Chapter 10

Recognizing "Real" Hellish Conditions

There are many across the divide of religious practices that talk about the concept of hell. None of them that I can recall speak of it in a positive way. That much everyone can agree upon. However, my discussion of it in this chapter does not focus on it as some far away distant place reserved for those who don't live their life a certain way. My take on it is much different. Hell for me is more akin to a state of powerlessness that leads to an inability to dictate your own emotional state. This has been a very big obstacle for me on the path. The inability to recognize what "hellish" conditions are does a very severe thing. It allows a person to believe that stressful situations are normal. Therefore, a person has no need to be free from them.

At the time of this writing I have recently gone thru a traumatic circumstance. Because of my practice of the teachings, I was able to process it differently than in times past. Although I still felt bad, the bad feeling was not because things had not gone my way. I felt bad because I did not like the fact that I was not able to control my emotional state. Let me say this loud and clear.

IT DOES NOT FEEL GOOD NOR IS IT A PLEASANT EXPEREINCE to have the world wind of emotions wreaking havoc on your emotional state. You have also likely experienced this as well. It is very difficult getting over unpleasant situations in life. Feeling bad about a situation and the associated feelings of a sense of loss, are not easy to handle. Combine this with the mental notions of wondering why this or that happened and whose fault it was creates an emotional state I would not wish on my enemy. This is a miserable state. This is the "hellish condition" to which this chapter refers. Feeling like this, and not being able to do anything about it, this is "hell," but many of us accept this way of being as normal because this is all we know. Even you as a student of the teachings prior to reaching the enlightened state will have times when you will have to deal with such "hellish conditions."

The problem though is that because the "hellish conditional state" is normal for most, realization that it is bad does not exist.

Consider the following example. A couple together for a couple of years breaks up. This is the circumstance that must be dealt with. Often people feel bad

"An Aspirant's Guide To Practicing The Egyptian Mysteries"

about the break-up and the sense of loss that comes with it. This is quite a bit to deal with by itself. But these questions and feelings don't end here. In fact they only begin here because a snowball effect is soon to occur. The snowball effect refers to how a small snowball rolling downhill gets larger and larger, the further downhill it goes. As it picks up speed it packs on more snow. For the person dealing with the break-up example, the following questions immediately also come to mind.

-What does this mean?
-Why is this person being this way?
-How come my life is not going the way I want it?
-How come I am not loved the way I want to be?

There are many more, and you can add in a few yourself. But these are the types of ideas that people get when they are in the emotional state (hell) and guess what? They cannot control it! Resultantly each one of these ideas leads to another idea which leads to another emotional state and so on and so on.

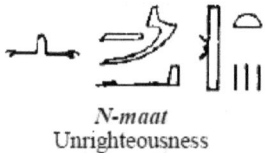

N-maat
Unrighteousness

For example the question "how come I'm not loved the way I want to be" can easily lead to feelings of inadequacy. Then new emotions come into being based upon the feeling of inadequacy. Now not only does the person feel bad about the original demise of the relationship, now they also feel bad about feeling inadequate. Feelings of inadequacy easily lead to feelings of a woe is me mindset, which then lead to the "why can't I ever be happy feeling?"

The associated feelings that derive from the new negative emotions create layers upon layers that now have to be dealt with. Every question mentioned above and others that come up leads to an additional emotion that now has to be dealt with. Before you know it, one issue becomes five or ten and the person easily becomes an emotional basket case. This is a "hellish" condition far worse than anything imagined in any religious tradition to which I am familiar. The one so called "bad moment" leads to an avalanche of associated thoughts which give rise to another avalanche of negative emotional feelings and we feel miserable. None of this is pleasant to deal with, but it is considered as normal for the vast majority of people.

Only thru my practice of the teachings of Shetaut Neter have I been able to realize that it is not the specific circumstances that are the problem, the break up in the example above, but instead it is the "way of being" in how we practice this thing called life. In fact, as a result of my practice of the teachings, I now realize that WE create our own "hellish conditions" and emotional states. The following example will show you how.

I recall when I was in high school I had a teacher that I will call Mr. Martin. I remember that he used to play mind games with the students in our class. Often during the semester I was in his class, it was quite normal to have him say something that would have the girls literally crying, that emotionally drove them to tears. It was also normal for him to say something to the guys that would make them get so mad and upset that they would storm out of class, short of being ready to hit someone including him. Mr. Martin would always say things which pushed people's buttons one way or another, and to me he seemed like he enjoyed it.

He never got to me in that kind of way though. I always watched and observed and never put myself in a position for me to get upset. But after a while, I did wonder what point he was trying to make in providing instruction in this way. And one day while I sat in that 12th grade senior high school classroom, I heard him say the following words. "If I can make you laugh, and if I can make you cry, I can control you, because I can dictate and control your emotional state." He then went on to explain how he wanted us to get ready for life as adults, and how we needed to be able to understand parts of ourselves that we did not know about. Needless to say, this blew me away. I had "never" thought about the concept of emotional states like this at any point in my life up to then.

Although blown away by it at first, I was not able to fully comprehend what he was saying. Back then I thought he was just mean and just liked getting thrills by making people upset. I thought he was ego tripping actually. But now as I have grown older and my practice of the teachings of Shetaut Neter have matured, I now have a much better understanding of what he was saying and teaching us.

Each one of my classmates who blew up emotionally when Mr. Martin pushed their button was in hell. Although they did not realize it, this is exactly where they were. Why? **Because someone else other than them was controlling their emotional state!** It really was hell too. When my classmates were upset, they were really upset. It was not fake. They felt terrible and it took awhile for them to come back around and get back to normal. Whatever individual process they had for getting over their upset or anger issue, they had to go thru. That's not an easy thing to do. Overcoming some type of adverse situation can be very difficult and emotionally draining.

As I graduated and left high school, I no longer had Mr. Martin attempting to push my buttons in an effort to control my emotional state. But that didn't matter because unbeknownst to me, I unconsciously replaced him with someone else known as my ego, which I will call Mr. Set. Over the course of my life my ego unconsciously became my own Mr. Martin and for most of it I did to something to myself he never could. Control me by controlling my emotional state! According to Mr. Martin, being able to make a person laugh and cry was the key to being able to control them emotionally. So knowing what a person liked and disliked was the foundation for this control. In the course of my life my ego unconsciously decided what I liked and disliked about a variety of things. Therefore I was my own Mr. Martin. In my case my ego, Mr. Set, had made these choices for me. The only difference was that instead of Mr. Martin pushing my buttons, I gave this control to the world thru situations and circumstances instead. Therefore when something happened which my Ego, Mr. Set, had unconsciously or consciously decided previously was something to "like," of course I was happy. The opposite was also true when a situation presented itself that I did not like, which made me mad or sad. I was unhappy.

Consequently, these decisions about what I liked and disliked gave rise to the buttons which would later become "triggers" for either a happy or upset emotional state. So unbeknownst to me, over time, I created my own "hellish" emotional states. Unfortunately until I began my study of the teachings, I did not realize that I had become my own Mr. Martin by falling prey to my ego Mr. Set.

The present western societal mindset and culture which promotes the so-called ideal of living life for the purpose of satisfying sense pleasures and desires promotes the hellish internal mindset. This is because when life is lived for the pursuit of sense pleasures; each unconscious decision is made about what is pleasing (what can make you laugh), and what is not (what can make you cry). Therefore, life lived in this way unconsciously forces a person to become their own Mr. Martin by allowing their ego to be in control. As so many people adopt this way of living and thinking, very few ever realize what is exactly happening.

I can now say without apology that the worst conditions I have ever found myself to be in are "hellish" conditions. Even today I still find myself in them far more often than I would like. Realization of the process now allows me to be aware of how hellish they actually are. Until I became aware of what I have done to myself in this way, I was stuck. My friends back in school never realized when Mr. Martin was manipulating them emotionally. How could they when it took most of their energy to just deal with their problem at hand (being upset). So they never realized they were in hell because they had become used to it!

With a bit of practice, the ways in which we do this to ourselves has become clearer for me. This does not mean that I no longer find myself in hellish conditions. I still do. But now I recognize that my emotions have been manipulated and now I get a fervent distaste for allowing myself to be in this position. I do not like having to work through these feelings when I am feeling emotionally very bad about something or conversely very good about something else either. Any situation that presents itself to you in life is nothing more than a situation that if handled properly, will aid in your spiritual development and growth, nothing more and nothing less.

However, living life with a Mr. Martin mindset creates additional pain and suffering as a whirlwind of negative emotions and thoughts is created.
This "way of being" was and still is to a certain extent for me normal, because I have lived this way for so long. Hellish moments occur far more often than the so-called good moments. But thru the practice of the teachings of Shetaut Neter, the "hellish" normal state of being is moving way to one based upon contentment and peace, hotep, hetep, HTP.

With reflection I have found the "hellish" way of living to be quite miserable. Once my button is pushed in a so called good or bad way by outside forces, I am immediately at the mercy of those outside forces. This is why it is important to know why something is pleasing to you. It is also why it is important to know why other things are not. Giving thought to the process that has occurred which gives rise to either of these emotional states is necessary to free yourself from them. Consider this. Do the things that please you please everyone else in this world? Do the things that upset you upset everyone else in the world? If the answer to either of these questions is no, then is it really the circumstance or is it your idea about it that is pleasing or sad? This means it is relative.[4]

---

[4] See Chapter Ideas Shape Reality

If you don't know the answers to these questions, then you are setting yourself up for experiencing "hellish" conditions without realizing it. This is because a person believes as true those things that they have grown accustomed to liking or disliking. Without reflection and thought, it is easy to forget that likes and dislikes change. So believing in the fallacy of likes and dislikes is nothing more than creating a button, that when pushed, will send a person over the edge in a good or bad way.

One of the byproducts of studying the teachings of Shetaut Neter is the fact that with enough study and practice of the teachings, introspection of several areas of your life naturally takes place. Additionally, introspection on the things that are pleasing and not so pleasing to the person also unconsciously occurs. For me these lessons were never spelled out in any of the Pyramid or Coffin Texts. They were not found in the Pert M Heru. I didn't find them in the mythic stories of Asar, Aset and Heru or Lady Hetheru and Djehuti. This knowledge came about indirectly as a result of listening to all of these teachings, reflecting on all of them, and then meditating on them.

There are some of you who want to avoid at all costs having to deal with "hell" once they die. As a result of the teachings I no longer worry about that. I have my hands full figuring what buttons I have created so that they can no longer be pushed. This takes vigilance and effort. I no longer want to be in "hell" by allowing my own Mr. Martin/Mr. Set to control me. This keeps me busy enough. This is why enlightened consciousness is something to live for. Forget hell when I die. Hell while I am alive is quite enough!

Chapter 11

Lost in the World

"We are souls who have forgotten that we are souls as we interact in what we mistakenly believe to be matter!" (Time and Space)

Have you ever been driving, mistakenly made a wrong turn and found yourself miles away from where you wanted to go? If this has ever happened to you was the result that you got lost? Did you then need the assistance of someone else to help get you back on the right path?

This very event happened to me recently. I was taking my daughter to get her hair done and while following the map quest directions, went north instead of south. Unfortunately for me, I was in a rural area and the exits were quite a distance apart. So I had to drive a long way just to see where I was. Additionally, as I had written the directions down instead of printing them, I did not have exit numbers for the exit I was looking for. All I had was the names. So I had no way of knowing if I was going in the right direction except for waiting until the street name I was looking for came up. Before I realized that I was going the wrong way I had driven for at least 45 minutes.

To live a spiritual life, it is important to realize that it is more likely than not that you have become lost in the world and like me not realize until very late what has happened.

Being lost means that we get so caught up in the things that we do our attention becomes blind to the fact that we are souls interacting in what appears to be matter. When I have gotten lost like this it is often because I have gotten caught up with the multitude of things necessary for everyday survival that I forget everything else. I know this is so because this happens to me more often than I would like. It is not an isolated occurrence. Even after regular practice of the Shedy disciplines after a few years, it is still something that I have to work thru on a regular basis.

"To free the spirit, control the senses; the reward will be a clear insight."
-Ancient Kamitic Proverb

"An Aspirant's Guide To Practicing The Egyptian Mysteries"

For me getting "lost" happens in numerous ways. Generally it involves doing those things that I need to do in order to take care of myself and my family. Working and looking for better work, interacting with family and friends, and the numerous ways in which I fall prey to responding to external stimuli of the world. All of these circumstances make it easy to get caught up in the day to day moments of life. When I get caught up in these types of activities I totally "forget" my essential spiritual nature. In those moments I believe I am Lawrence Mathews. When I "forget" that I am spirit and think that I am Lawrence I am officially "lost in the world."

Unfortunately for me, just like when I was driving and did not realize I was going the wrong way until it was too late, most of the time I do not realize when I am lost in the world due to activity that takes my mind off my essential nature. Being lost in the world, forgetting our essential nature, is typical for non-aspirants and aspirants alike. For the non-aspirant being lost is the normal way of being. For the aspirant, being lost is an impediment to our growth and spiritual development. But how does a person know they are lost before it's late? In my driving example, who wants to travel 45 miles in the wrong direction before realizing their present circumstance?

Dr. Muata Ashby (Sebai Maa) speaks about why it is easy for all people to easily become "lost in the world." He has written the following as it relates to this dynamic.

"The Sages and Saints of Ancient Kamit have taught that the Divine Self is transcendental and absolute. Thus the Sun is the symbol used to represent the Divine Self because it is par excellent because it shines continuously. The Sun does not have light and dark like the earth. It is constantly full light, thus it transcends time and space. Likewise the Divine Self transcends changes in consciousness as it is absolute. This is unlike human beings, who change constantly from waking to dream and then sleep, from death to life and then to death, youth to old age, i.e., the changes of the opposites. In the Divine Self there are no opposites, only the singular transcendental essence.

When that singular essence is projected into time and space, individuated sparks of that Divine consciousness come into being. These sparks are the souls of human beings. When the projection occurs, a form of delusion occurs wherein the individuated ray of

"An Aspirant's Guide To Practicing The Egyptian Mysteries"

light forgets where it came from. Then it needs to be led back to the knowledge of the Divine Light, the Self, from where it came from and is."[5]

This means that the individuated ray of consciousness forgets that it is a soul and believes itself to be human instead. So the process of incarnation itself produces a form of delusion/forgetfulness of our essential spiritual nature. This is very important to realize because it tells us the level vigilance necessary to overcome this. Therefore the process of incarnation itself predisposes us to being "lost in the world." What took me awhile to grasp on the spiritual path was this predisposition fact. I did not immediately realize that through my consistent interaction in the world I would **regularly** become lost in it.

This is a big deal. When I was lost and driving in the wrong direction with my daughter, I DID NOT REALIZE I WAS LOST! Just like then, when I am caught up in the day to ritual, I DO NOT REALIZE THAT I AM LOST EITHER! How can I or anyone proceed on a path if they unknowingly are going in the wrong direction? For clarity sake understand that "attention" away from the Divine Self within with "exclusive" attention on day to day moment to moment activities constitutes being "lost in the world."

For ease of understanding be aware that it is not the activities performed that constitute being "lost in the world." It is where the person's "attention" is when engaged in the activity. The same activity can be done IF the inner attention of the person remains constantly on the Divine Self. This is why the teachings proscribe that an aspirant is to "spiritualize all of their actions." This keeps the "attention" within where it promotes spiritual growth and development.

When I was temporarily lost driving my daughter and also during those times I'm caught up in the world, you could say that a form of delusion had come over me in line in with what the Sages and Saints spoke of above. This delusion made me think that everything was fine. While on the road driving I think my daughter may have even said to me at one point that she thought we might be going the wrong way. I didn't listen to her and dismissed her comments. I mean what did she know about where we were supposed to be going?

---

[5] From the Book, "The Glorious Light Meditation, By Dr. Muata Ashby pg. 19

Be careful when getting caught up in the day to grind of living. It is very easy for your attention to be focused on everything but your essential spiritual nature. Forgetting who you are can easily happen like this. When this happens to me what I need is someone to fill the role my daughter played who can tell me that I am going the wrong way. This in our tradition is normally the Spiritual Preceptor or Teacher. It can even be a Priest/Priestess or another aspirant. It can even be the scriptures themselves. The only thing that needs to be done is that this person/teaching must be listened to and heeded when the "right" directions are given.

Do not think that the way the words in this chapter express this idea makes "finding" oneself after being "lost" a simple proposition. Although conceptually it could be said that it is a simple process, our Spiritual Preceptor Sebai Maa has told us previously, "Something that is simple does not mean that it is easy!"

There have been many times as an initiate that I have completely forgotten my essential spiritual nature. Even while studying the teachings on a regular basis. This happens because until a person fully identifies with the spiritual essence of their being, they will always have to deal with the magnetic pull of the world as it calls our name thru our senses.

The ego (Set) has the senses working for it to keep control over the personality. They are a very strong team and consistently defeat those not actively engaged in the spiritual practice. They are so strong in fact that they also defeat the initiate until a certain level of detachment has occurred in that personality. For me it is very easy to get lost in what I see, hear, taste, touch and smell on a regular basis. This is even easier as western societal culture places significant value on those things we interact with thru these means. Consequently for me, placing significant value on the spiritual nature instead of what the senses perceive can be more than a notion.

> "Knowledge derived from the senses is illusionary, true knowledge can only come from the understanding of the union of the opposites."
> -Ancient Kamitic Proverb

Identification with reality that exists beyond the senses cannot be attained until a person has "experienced" the transcendental realm on a regular basis. This is done thru the regular Shedy practice and advanced stages in the meditative process. Before this identification could occur for me on a regular basis a couple things needed to happen. First I needed to become aware of the degree to which I "valued" those things I interacted with daily thru my senses. Next, I had to practice the Shedy disciplines long enough to realize that the senses do not provide an accurate perception of what reality is. These realizations were the key because as long as I consciously or unconsciously placed ANY abiding value on what was perceived in this way, I was/am still prone to getting "lost in the world."

Even though I still struggle with getting "lost in the world," (forgetting my essential spiritual nature) now that I am aware of how this process occurs, I am much better at determining when I made a wrong turn and hence driving the wrong way. This has been an important lesson for me in the past and is just as important today. Hopefully it will help you as well. I mean who wants to be "lost" anywhere? Especially in the world?

Ba ir pet Shat ir ta
"Soul is to heaven, body is to the earth"
From the Prt m Hru of the *Pyramid Texts* (3,200-2,575 B.C.E.)

Chapter 12

And the World Comes Tumbling Down!

Quite often in my life I have had occasion to believe that having a particular thing; car, money, or relationship would make me "feel" a particular way. Happy, content and fulfilled best describe how I thought these things would make me "feel." Even in the career/job area, I believed that the achievement of my goals would be fulfilling. For me the "reality" of how I felt upon getting those things was always disappointing. The "glitter" was always much better than the "gold." The total mental acceptance that obtainment of particular objects do not provide complete fulfillment is part (a) of how my world has begun to start tumbling down. Part (b) is what mental acceptance of this idea has done to my overall idea about what life is and how it is to be lived.

To obtain Nehast in this lifetime, a practitioner of the teachings must ready him/her self for a 360 degree mental shift. A person's mental view of what the world is and how to interact in it will soon be changing. Unfortunately this change happens incrementally. Not surprisingly realization of this change is often missed. Nevertheless, for the daily practitioner, a new mind "set" is taking hold. The old mind "set" in a previous way begins to be "purified" which brings forth a new mind "set." When the purified mind begins to replace the older mind, the practitioner's world has officially begun to tumble down.

To some this may sound like a good thing. Purification of the mind seems to be something that all would find pleasing. Who wouldn't want to cleanse something that is dirty that can be cleansed? But based upon my own individual practice, although purification originally sounded good to me also, I did not immediately embrace letting go of my old mind "set." This is because I knew how things were in the old way of thinking but had no idea about how things would be in the "clean" purified mental state.

Although Nehast sounds good as a goal, (and of course its achievement is the purpose of life) it is a concept that cannot be held or grasped in one's hand. It is not concrete so it cannot be called and spoken to. It cannot be prepared and be eaten a variety of ways. It

cannot be lived in or driven. It cannot be spent. I have associated happiness, contentment and fulfillment with the obtainment of those "things" that I could experience in these ways. However, Nehast which promises the exact same results, happiness, contentment and complete fulfillment except in a "perpetual" way, cannot be experienced like this. In fact, this experience occurs without the use of the senses at all.

For me this was internally the roughest aspect to my practice of the teachings. How could I experience something without the use of my senses? For me, I didn't even think that there was an existence beyond them. I remember saying to myself, "Now I have to learn how to experience life in this way even though I had no clue previously that I could?" This question resonated within me for quite awhile. So I thought, "I have to leave a concrete form of interaction of life through the use of my senses and replace it with one that cannot be experienced or described with words! Needless to say that although my words said I wanted Nehast, my old mind "set" didn't want anything like this. It wanted to "hold" onto all it knew which was the belief that this old mind "set" was concrete and real. Therefore letting go of this old mind was not easy. But it is letting go of this old mind which makes a practitioner's world begin to start tumbling down.

One thing that is noticed incrementally as the practice of the teachings is done consistently is what intermittent happiness, joy, and peace is. Something that is intermittent occurs occasionally. It comes and then it goes. In my lifetime I had grown accustomed to the intermittent nature of all of these things. For me they all were quite normal. So although the teachings promise a "perpetual and abiding" peace, joy and contentment, I really had no context to understand what this looked like and was. Resultantly the context for letting go of the desire for anything that was intermittent was difficult.

Based upon my study and practice, I now understand that to achieve Nehast in this lifetime one of the things that must be done is to have a shift in consciousness. In other words, a person has to learn how to "shift" what they are consciously aware of. This starts the process of bringing forth the Anpu quality which allows one to be able to discern and tell the difference between what is real and unreal. At first glance this may seem pretty simple. However, it is anything but that. Right now

for most, we are only conscious of those things that appear to exist in our outer world. The things we experience through our senses which allow us to see, taste, touch, feel and hear. We are also conscious of our emotional state/s. This is so because emotions come into existence after something has been experienced by our senses. Our consciousness is concentrated on everything that exists "outside" of us.

So we look "out" into the world and are conscious of those things that we interact with in this way.

But there is quite more to existence than what we experience in this way. Air, sun rays, gravity, and energy, just to name a few, are a small number of things that exist outside the purview of our outer experience. We are oblivious to these things because our consciousness is not shifted on them. Resultantly we give little credence if any to the "reality" of their existence not because they are illusory but because we are not consciously aware of them. But can anyone live without air? What type of existence would there be if there was no gravity? Clearly lack of conscious awareness of something does not mean that it does not exist.

The conscious "shift" of attention/awareness away from the outer aspect of a person to the inner, is what the everyday practice of the teachings is designed to do. This shift over time allows the practitioner to see how unfulfilling intermittent anything actually is.

For me, at the beginning, this "shift" was so subtle that I didn't realize that a shift was taking place. Looking back on it I can now see how the shift started. As the "shift" progression continued, a point was reached where I began to realize that existence really is composed of more than just what I had previously only known through the use of my senses.

This consciousness shift is a wonderful thing and is the goal of all religious traditions whether its practitioners realize it or not. Then, it is realized that the "inner world," only appeared to be illusory and imaginary simply because the practitioner was not paying attention (conscious) to it. Therefore, awareness of this aspect of existence is what was lacking. Not its existence.

Awareness and attention is the consciousness shift that I am referring to. It is this consciousness shift away from the outer world experienced through the senses that causes a person's outer world to come tumbling down. The belief in the inherent so called reality of the outer world falls and tumbles down. This process is welcomed and can be easy for some. For others it can pose many challenges. I was/am one that it posed many challenges for.

For a reason I still find hard to explain, no matter how many times I became frustrated and/or disappointed "after" I received something I thought would make me happy, I kept on looking for other things. When I graduated from college and thought that buying myself a car would make me happy I did so. Very soon the novelty wore off of that object and I wanted another one. So then I focused my "attention" on another object. This time it was the job of my dreams. So I spent more time and energy putting myself in a position for that. Upon receipt of this job of my dreams, the novelty again soon wore off. Not long after that, I wanted another type of job. Next it was the woman of my dreams. More time and energy was expended in meeting and getting to know this person. Once I had the woman of my dreams and we became involved in the relationship, the novelty again wore off and I found that maybe someone else was actually a better woman for me.

You would think that after a certain point I would have realized that this way of living life was not working. The only thing I consistently got was let down. Another way of saying this is that I was consistently frustrated and disappointed. Unfortunately for me this was not the case. I now see that I couldn't stop this way of living because I was afraid to have my world come tumbling down. Although objectively this way of living life was not good for me and wasted a lot of time, this was all that I knew. Therefore I was reluctant to let go of this way of thinking. Frankly, I did not know any other way existed. Even as my practice continued over the years, letting go of this mindset was very difficult. Even as I write these words, there are areas of my life where I still internally want to believe that the "right" job or the "right" person will make everything all "right!"

Wrong! ☺ This way of living produces the same outcomes it always has. These are frustration and discontent. However even to this

day in some areas of my life I am still reluctant in allowing my belief in the outer world to come down. Because I am so attached to the belief in some "right thing or person" I still find it difficult to let this belief go. Therefore it's easy to "forget" about the other "inner world" where consciousness needs to be shifted to. Attachment to the old mind "set" makes it easy to get impatient with the practice of "shifting" my consciousness. In the old way of thinking, at some point you "get" something.

However, when consciousness shifts inward, there is no immediate gratification like we currently know. Although the foundation for being able to rise above the pettiness of life has begun to take root, this is so subtle that it cannot be fully realized. At least for me I couldn't at first.

But in due time and due season, you will be able to see the fruits of your labor. The shift of consciousness from the outer world to the inner world is something that must be "experienced." The more it is experienced, the more you will begin to "know" it. The more you "know" it, the easier it will be to deal with life's issues. These issues will start becoming "petty" and your ability to deal with them free of emotional attachment will provide you with a form of peace that you have not had before. This is what happens as the outer world tumbles down. Lost are the reasons for being disappointed and frustrated. Lost are the reasons for being angry or upset. What is found is the answer to the age old question who am I. It is this answer that completely destroys the belief in the inherent so called reality of the outer world. It is this answer that allows you to see the underlying essence that is behind all of creation and how that same essence is nothing other than YOU! In our tradition it is the reason for living and the purpose of life. To "experience" the inner aspect of ourselves so much that we identify this as reality and the human so called experience as illusory. When this happens the practitioner can officially say that their world has tumbled down.

"An Aspirant's Guide To Practicing The Egyptian Mysteries"

SET

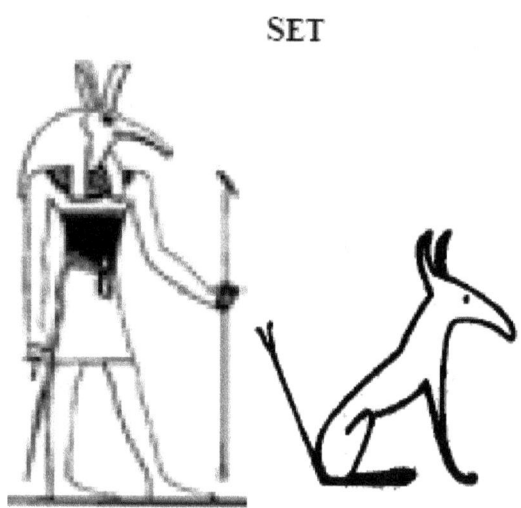

Chapter 13

Holding Onto the World of Mental Agitation

When I initially began studying mystical philosophy and religion, I often heard people discuss the importance of letting go of the world. For me this was simply a matter of letting go of my idea that reality as viewed thru the lens of my senses was accurate. Intellectually this seemed simple enough. Basic elementary school science taught me that everything at its essence is composed of atoms and that atoms at their core are mostly empty space/energy. Therefore it did not seem like making this mental transition would be all that difficult. How wrong I was!

It has now been approximately ten years since I began seriously studying the teachings of Shetaut Neter. Time has changed what my initial idea on what "letting go of the world" means. This is especially true in a practical sense. Although the intellectual understanding as enumerated above has not changed and is still valid, the application to it in everyday settings has. As a neophyte and prophyte practitioner of the teachings, I was not aware of the unconscious mental ways that I actually "hold onto" the world everyday. This presented a quandary. How can I let go of something if I don't first know how to recognize exactly what I am holding onto?

It is has been said that the practice of the teachings liberates and frees the practitioner from ideas and beliefs that make them feel small and limited. This "liberation" also initially sounded wonderful. But it led to another quandary. How am I bound to these ideas and thoughts in everyday life in the first place? How would freedom from this bondage look? What is it that is keeping me in bondage that I need "freedom" from? Answering these questions is the subject of this chapter.

To get a feel for how we are unconsciously mentally bound, consider spending one hour or less observing yourself as you interact with the world in the regular course of your day. Watch yourself as you go thru your daily routine of life. Notice where your eyes take you as you walk down the street. Notice how your body feels when you encounter certain situations. Notice how you blurt out certain things in spite of not wanting to. Everything you observe as you do this exercise is a small way in which we both hold onto the world and it holds onto us.

Contrast this with Sages and enlightened personalities who also walk down the street and look at things. These personalities unlike us are not affected by the external stimulus. This is because they no longer perceive the objects in Creation as separate and individuated. They see the underlying unity that gives rise to and supports all that appears to exist. Only a person who perceives things separate can want to have union with that other thing. This union can be the eating of food, a relationship with another person, even holding a flower because it makes you allegedly feel good. Therefore, Sages have nothing to hold onto because they internally "know" that their essence is the exact same as the object being perceived.

Although you may be intellectually attempting to practice balance, harmony, truth and justice in your life (Maat), this practice initially easily gives way to appeals from the senses which remind us of previous experiences. This is because our minds have grown accustomed to interpreting data received by our senses a certain way. Certain events elicit a "happy" response. Others elicit a "sad" one. Objects are interpreted as being "real" and abiding. Additionally "ari" also known as karma moves us to act out in ways beyond what is in our best interest. All of this makes practicing the precepts of Maat on a daily basis challenging. All of these are ways that we hold onto the world and never realize it.

As a beginning and intermediate student of the teachings, I was not immune to falling prey to the "unconscious impressions/ari" of the sense pleasures. Even today, as an advanced student, I still wrestle with certain urges. Whenever a person acts in accordance with an urge based upon a sense pleasure desire, that person is allowing the world to control them. Fortunately, time has allowed me to become aware of many of these urges. Now that they have become conscious, I am better able to deal with them. Unfortunately, I still fall prey to some of them. However, I also now recognize that this is okay as long as I learn from the experience, move on, and work on not allowing it to happen again.

What Are We Holding Onto That We Need Freedom From? Mental Agitation!

The so called "normal" way of living life has a person mentally juggling several ideas while simultaneously juggling several actions. This is a way in which we hold onto the world. The mind of a person like this is ALWAYS in a constant state of motion. Many today have gotten so used to this way of being, that some say that they feel good operating in this way. Others consider this as normal and accept it as a state experienced by all who are human. Even conversations with others go from one thing to the next without a semblance of balance or order. This convoluted way of living life makes it easy to see why people go to sleep at night thinking about what they did not do, dream about what they have to do, and wake up worried about what they forgot to do. This is an example of mental agitation. Rarely if ever does a person engage in a thought or activity in a concentrated and focused way.

Mental agitation is present when there is constant movement of the mind from one thought to another. It is also present when there is constant movement of the mind from one extreme (happiness) to the other (sadness). Mental agitation also appears when there is longing for life circumstances to be different than they actually are. Because many of us do not know any better, many of us hold onto the world in this way (mental agitation) and think this is normal.

Many people have become so used to this agitation that they cannot operate any other way. It is safe to say that many have become addicted to having restless agitated minds. This is one of the reasons why there is such a high level of stress in the world today. Although some consider constant mental movement normal, our bodies do not. It should not be surprising to see the large number of people dying at younger and younger ages of stress related issues.

A mind accustomed to constant mental agitation can also be called a "heavy mind." This makes sense because the more things placed into any type of container, (the mind is a container of thoughts, ideas, etc) the heavier that container will be. Many people do not see an agitated mind as heavy, not because of the weight, but because they have carried it so long they have become immune to noticing it.

Objectively speaking, having a "heavy mind" would not seem like something worthy of desire. Living life like this on a regular basis appears to be something that a person would want to avoid. But many do not know what mental agitation is, let alone know of another way of living life. Resultantly, we hold onto this agitation. For me in certain areas of my life I absolutely refused to let this mental agitation go. In some ways, it was my crutch.

For example I have spoken previously about how for much of my life, my dislike of my father was my motivation for being different from him. Holding onto the agitation of dislike gave me strength to be different from him. I used this mental agitation to motivate me. Although I turned out okay, the stress I put on myself was not worth it. To this day, I still discover certain areas of my life where I have thoughts and ideas that I still hold onto which lead to mental upset-ness and discontent. It is a constant process of discovery.

However, the practice of the teachings has allowed me to get "glimpses" of the mental plane beyond where agitation resides. These glimpses over time add up and eventually lead a person to having a concentrated/lucid mind. The more the mind is concentrated, the more it is able to experience itself with "no thoughts versus having a mind with many thoughts."

Experiencing No Thoughts

In our tradition a term called Nrutf is described as the unconscious plane of existence. It is also described as "the place where nothing grows." For purposes of this chapter, it is a description of a mind that is still and free from the voluminous unwanted thoughts and imaginations that people have. In its properly understood context, *nrutf* is not to be considered the unconscious mind per se- it is a region of it, a region deeper, beyond the level of thoughts, like a deep dark black hole, and above and outside the hole are the seeds of thought, the ari, beyond (above) that there are the clouds, of many forms, the thoughts (subconscious) blown around by the winds of desires and feelings, beyond that are the thoughts of current attention, the conscious mind. The experience of this plane over prolonged periods of time helps a person let go of the world/mental agitation.

Through the Integrated Sheti practice, in time, you will experience "glimpses" of the "no thought" way of being. These "glimpses" will occur during the meditative practice. After a certain period, these glimpses will grow longer in length and duration and will start to be "remembered" by your personality/ego. The more they happen, the easier it will be to remember them.

During this process, you will discover an indescribable feeling of freedom. For me this freedom was something that I had not experienced previously. It was this/these experiences which allowed me to understand what I had been holding onto. It was these experiences that allowed me to "know" what mental agitation really was/is. These longer "glimpse" periods allowed me to experience the "lightness" of a lucid mind. I needed this so that I could know how "heavy" the dull and agitated mind that I had really was.

Letting go of the world for me was difficult because I did not fully understand that mental agitation is itself what I was holding onto. Let go of the world, and the world will let go of you.

"An Aspirant's Guide To Practicing The Egyptian Mysteries"

SET

Heru

Chapter 14

THE HOLY WAR WITHIN
The Battle of Heru and Set in the Everyday Practical World

If you have not yet read the Asarian Myth and Resurrection story, you soon will. It is important to read this myth, and then reflect and meditate on it for understanding of its deeper mystical implications. There is much to the story, and there are many characters in it. Suffice it to say that the entire story is a reflection of the predicament of the human soul of every person once it incarnates, and the struggle it encounters as it subsequently forgets its eternal essence. Most importantly, the myth shows the process necessary for the soul to "remember" its divine nature and how to rise above life's challenges.

Asar

This chapter centers on the part of the myth when the battle between Heru and his uncle Set takes place. Heru is the son of Asar. Asar was killed by his brother Set. At the time of his death, Asar was the King of Egypt. Heru as his son was the rightful heir to the throne. After killing Asar, Set usurped the throne when Heru was a child. As a child Heru was taught by his spiritual preceptor mother Aset, and after growing older, decided to confront his uncle Set to take back the throne which rightfully belonged to him. It is the movement and twists and turns that happen when this confrontation takes place that is the subject of this chapter. It is a battle between the part of you that is used to doing things the way you have been doing them all of your life (your lower nature-Set) and the part of you that is now resurrecting your father (your soul) which is known as aspiration (Heru).

Heru represents that aspect of your personality (your higher consciousnesses) that has begun focusing your attention inward towards the Divine, and away from the outer exterior of the world. It is the aspect of you that now wants Nehast/Enlightenment.

There is a problem though. Enlightenment is not a one time event. It involves a process of cleansing and purification which allows us to realize the underlying essence which we already are. With dedicated effort, the time necessary to achieve this state can be a short one. However, each of us is different and the amount of effort and time needed in the purification process in this lifetime is different for each. It is the process of cleansing that gives rise to "the holy war within" that is the title of this chapter.

The Battle Within

The Spiritual movement is one that goes up and down. Some days you will feel as if you are making great progress. On these days your desires for the world will not be strong. When these days present themselves, it will be easy or not that difficult to abstain from eating meat, to not curse, or to not have a drink of wine with dinner. On these days it will also be easier to do your Sheti Practices three times a day. When this happens, you will notice that your willpower will be very strong. But on the other days, your desires will be far different. On these days, you may have friends who will offer you meals with meat even though they know you are a vegetarian. At the beginning there will be days when you will actually want a piece of that meat. You will have days when you won't feel like getting up in the morning to do your prayers, chants and meditations. And on some days don't be surprised if you will want objects in the world as a means to be "happy" even though you know intellectually that the acquisition of these objects will not provide the happiness you seek.

Until spiritual awakening has occurred, be mindful of two types of battles which you may experience. The first battle occurs during the first few years at the beginning when you start a consistent practice of teachings that lead to "awakening" (Nehast). The second battle occurs after you have had some time in your practice but before spiritual liberation happens. This could be five years or more after you have studied and practiced the teachings consistently. It is likely that these battles will take form in the following ways:

1. Inability to Control Desire,
2. Relationships,
3. Judging Spiritual Progress,
4. Having More Adversity In Life Than Before (job loss, family loss or issues).

Be mindful that not everyone will experience the same type of experiences. Some experiences may be easier than those experienced by someone else. Those that have an easier time will do so because of their *ari*. Those that have a more difficult time will do so because of their *ari*. In the book "The Wisdom of Maat," by Dr. Muata Ashby, the concept of *ari* is described as follows:

"An Aspirant's Guide To Practicing The Egyptian Mysteries"

"Actions are called ari. Ones actions leave impressions in the unconscious mind and these later emerge as desires which impel the personality to certain situations."

Ari
"Action," "to do something," "things done"
(From Chapter 33 of the *Prt m Hru*)

Recently in a conversation with Dr. Muata Ashby (Sebai Maa), he had this to say about *Ari:*

"Ari is a sum total of past feelings, desires and actions – that sum total is like a seed of desire, a residue, and attached to that desire is a portion of Sekhem, energy/force to implement it; the energy force associated with it is in proportion to the amount of reinforcement by the person to whom the ari belongs – it is that accumulated reinforcement (due to weak, medium, strong desire, etc.) that produces a force which impels or compels the person to act on that ari. A person may diffuse the energy (through spiritual disciplines) and still have the desire-though at that point the desire is manageable since the force has been diffused. A person may dispel the desire and still have the energy- that needs to be redirected, etc. Both latter cases are the objectives, with the ultimate goal of dispelling illusions, freeing up energy and redirecting it towards disciplines- especially meditation and transcendence."

According to *A Concise Encyclopedia of Hinduism*, by Klaus K. Klostermaier, it is defined as:

"the residue or mental impression of any action performed by an unenlightened person."

This residue remains with a person even after death due to the person's desire to experience pleasure from their performance of the action, because of spiritual ignorance. So your ability to quickly be able to benefit from the teachings of Shetaut Neter, or your ability to need more time of reflection and study of it, are

119

directly dependent upon the residue/impressions in your unconscious mind which have followed you into this lifetime from previous ones.

1. Inability to Control Desire

The first battle is the conflict between having a desire for something in the world when you now know intellectually that its fulfillment will not provide perpetual happiness or contentment. This is difficult because your ego will express this desire through a "feeling" that you have gotten for many years of your life. You will want a Big Mac just because you do. You will want a beer just because you do. You may talk to that attractive woman or man because you just want to know that you still "got it." This "feeling" is a direct reflection of previous immediate responses to your unpurified instinct. For much of your life prior to studying the teachings, you have trained yourself to act on these instincts. In fact, you have practiced this so much that you have become very proficient at it. Many people do not realize that there is a difference between their instinct and intellect. Do not be surprised or alarmed if you have more moments of falling prey to your instincts than you would like. Just keep track of how long it takes you to recognize what happened. The more you practice, the faster your recognition will be. The increased recognition time is a sign of spiritual progress.

NEBETHET

Be mindful that with your study and practice of the teachings, you are allowing an important thing to happen. First, you are allowing your unpurified instinct to become purified. The instinct is known as the Anpu faculty and it allows you to understand the difference between what is real and what is not real. The Anpu faculty (purified instinct) opens the way to awakening your wisdom and intuitional faculties. Both the wisdom and intuitional aspects of the personality are known as Aset. Development of love for the Divine leads to intuitional experience of the Divine. It is this experience which leads to Nehast.

Aset

As all of these faculties grow, you will become able to look at your previous actions objectively for the first time. Intellectually it is now much easier to see that previous actions done to achieve happiness in the past do not work over long periods of time.

As you read the myth you will become aware of how the characters in the myth relate to you as an aspirant. Your previous emotion/sense pleasure way of being led in life is Set, and your new point of view is Heru, assisted by wisdom and intuition which as discussed earlier is Aset. The holy war is the struggle between reacting to life's circumstances based upon your understanding and practice of the teachings instead of the way you have done in the past, the old way representing the way led by the ego with an unpurified instinct.

Every reaction to each life circumstance will be different. Some previous unpurified instinctual reflexes will subside quickly as your Sheti practice intensifies and as your meditation practice deepens. But there are others that have left a larger impression (Ari). These areas will not subside overnight. They will take time and effort to work through.

There will be moments when you will defeat the ego and just as many others when you won't. Don't get too up or down emotionally depending upon the situation. Take heed and know that this is a part of the process.

The second battle when dealing with the attempt to control desire occurs after you have studied the teachings for a prolonged period of time and prior to reaching spiritual liberation. This battle is very subtle. It manifests as a feeling of discontent and even frustration when, after practicing the teachings for years, you realize that you still have desires in the world. The frustration here is not about the battle between the worldly desires and rising above them. This is a battle based upon the belief that you should not be having worldly desires anymore. You will know this is happening when you hear yourself say things such as, "I should be further along than this, or I shouldn't be having these types of desires anymore."

These types of comments are borne from the deep conviction that you want Nehast in this lifetime. The frustration here is not frustration from having to battle your ego because of a worldly desire. It is from feeling like you should be further along than you think you are. This is a very subtle way that Set attempts to move us away from the path of Nehast. The ego will not easily stop its efforts to prevent its loss of control over the personality of a person. Self criticism about ones' efforts is a sure way to make worldly desires become appealing again. "Why keep practicing after all these years?" you may find yourself saying, "I'm still in the same place I was before. If I'm not making progress, these teachings must not work!"

TRUST THE PROCESS and understand that these feelings are normal. See yourself as Heru and know that as he won the battle in the end, so will you if you don't give up.

2. Relationships

By far the most difficult aspect of the ego to be faced as an aspirant is that part dealing with the desire to be in a relationship with someone of the opposite or same sex (depending on their sexual preference). The desire is strong because it is believed that a relationship will bring a person "happiness." It doesn't matter whether a person is single or married; this desire is so strong that it can render a person helpless to it. The desire can be likened to the following example. Consider being completely broke with absolutely no money, not even a penny, for more than a year. Then all of sudden someone with wealth unknowingly drops their wallet. The wallet is filled with cash so thick it is bulging. The person who dropped the wallet doesn't notice that they have lost it, but you do. Based on where you're standing, all you have to do is walk slowly over to the wallet, drop a bag or piece of clothing on top it, pick it up and keep going. There's only one problem. Your conscience is telling you not to do it, while your mind being ruled by your ego is telling you the opposite. Deep down inside you know that you shouldn't take it. But you've had no money for so long that this opportunity seems like it will never come again.

So you take the wallet. You have had ideas about having money for so long that you take it without giving serious thought to doing otherwise. In the example above it seems like there was a dilemma. In the practical world there is no dilemma. The "feeling/desire" to take the wallet is so strong that it overpowers any righteous thought. The soul becomes a bystander and watches as you drop your coat over the wallet, pick it up, and keep on walking.

This is a *minute* example of the level of desire experienced by a person when attracted to someone they are interested in. When engaged in the societal courtship rituals, the desire is much stronger than this. People in the world cannot control this desire. In fact, I believe it is safe to say that many people are slaves to it. Beginning aspirants who study the teachings of Shetaut Neter usually cannot control this desire either. Time and understanding of what drives the desire is needed before a person can begin exerting control over it. Few advanced aspirants of the teachings can fully control this desire. Many of them also fall prey to it. It's very challenging for either of these groups to control this energy as the energy compelling them to act can be likened to the force from the waves of a Tsunami (ariu-impression). When the ocean waves come ashore (sex desire), all that can be done for a person is to get out of the way.

According to our teachings, *Ari* as stated previously, is the sum total of past feelings, desires and actions of a person. Attached to it is an amount of Sekhem/life force energy. The amount of this force is dependent upon the level of reinforcement of the original feeling, desire or action, in the first place. The greater the reinforcement, the greater the force. In the example above regarding desire for the opposite sex, this desire is reinforced in many ways. Conversations with our peers about how wonderful being with a member of the opposite sex can be reinforce the desire and produces Sekhem energy. The music played on the radio and the movies that are shown also do the same thing. This energy from the reinforcement of each feeling, desire, and action, builds up over time in the unconscious part of our mind. After awhile it becomes so strong that it compels a person to act. No matter what the situation or circumstance, this energy has built up so strongly, that a person becomes helpless to do anything else. As stated previously, *Ari* carries over from lifetime to lifetime. *Ari* is cleansed by the practice of the Shedy disciplines which include meditation, transcendence and culminates in Nehast. *Ari* can be of good impressions that compel one to good actions or of negative impressions which lead a person to act in very egoistic ways thus creating more negative *ari no* matter what type it is, *ari* must be eradicated.

One reason that a battle between Heru and Set occurs is because "awareness" of the feelings, actions and desires mentioned above is now dawning. For the beginning and advancing aspirant, everyday they practice the teachings, they become more "aware" of the "ariu/impressions" driving their decision making. For the ordinary person, no awareness exists. Therefore, there is nothing to battle as they act based upon an unpurified instinct. Although decisions made in this way rarely turn out in a positive light, this person does not ever change, because this is all they know. However, for the aspirant engaged in the process of purifying their personality, they become more and more aware of those things which push their buttons.

It should not be surprising to have this play out as a battle. Awareness (in this example on the desire to be with a member of the opposite sex), now gives the aspirant something to think about or consider. Prior to purification efforts, there was no such thing. Now the impulse to act in the same way over the course of this

and previous other lifetimes comes face to face with your understanding that the impulse is not "real." Although we "feel" the impulse mentally and even physically, as aspirants we begin to "know" that it is illusionary. Until we "fully know" this desire is not real, it plays itself out in a battle between your intellect and wisdom faculties versus your personality/ego.

It is through purification of the personality and the wisdom teachings represented by Aset that the aspirant will be able to overcome this force in due time and due season. This will not happen overnight. It takes practice and mental fortitude. There will be more than a few occasions in which you will fall prey to the desire, that woman looks so good, that all of a sudden you start talking to her. Even when she tells you she has five kids by two dads and lives with her boyfriend, you take her phone number anyway. Even when that man tells you that he hasn't worked an actual job in five years but has been building his music career and he has five kids by three different women, you give him your phone number anyway.

Fortunately as an aspirant (depending upon the intensity and level of your practice), your ability to regain your composure will come back to you before you become entangled with this person. As *ari* works in positive ways also, living life based upon Maat creates a reservoir of positive impressions. These positive *ariu* helps us move beyond the initial desire filled ego reaction so that we can look clearly at how interaction with this person in any way other than a platonic one makes no sense.

Aset

As stated previously a person not practicing the teachings has a very small chance at controlling this force. Resultantly, the force of this desired relationship quickly leads to a host of problems which may create a lifetime of entanglements to deal with (children, divorce, jail if domestic violence occurs etc.).

3. Having More Adversity in Life Today Than You Had Prior to the Study of the Teachings

The teachings make it clear that suffering and adversity in life are a part of the fabric upon which Creation is built. The teachings are clear on this. No one escapes experiencing some sort of pain and adversity. An Egyptian Proverb makes this clear.

"To suffer is a necessity entailed upon your nature, would you prefer that miracles should protect you from its lessons or shalt you repine, because it happened unto you, when lo it happened unto all? Suffering is the golden cross upon which the rose of the Soul unfolds."

On a practical level knowing that we have to experience adversity does not provide consolation when it knocks at our door. Depending upon the individual circumstance, this knowledge may seem to make it worse. On a deeper level, we have learned that pain, suffering and adversity are nothing more than illusions. The deeper meaning behind the teachings of Shetaut Neter allows us to understand the "illusionary nature" of Creation. Intellectually it is not difficult to receive this. However, applying this to everyday life is quite a different story.

Inherent in the practice of living life spiritually is the belief that things in life should somehow get better now that we have started to study the teachings. This mistaken idea if not handled carefully can be the cause of great adversity and pain. This can occur because if you haven't yet, you will soon realize that both are self created.

Although the preceptor, teacher, or teachings have not and do not say this, more often than not, we believe that negative circumstances in life should go away when we begin living life more spiritually. This belief makes it easy to "feel" like areas in your life are much worse than they were before you began studying the teachings.

At the time of this writing, the USA is experiencing one of the worst economic times since the Great Depression of the late 1920's and early 1930's. There are many people with college degrees, even advanced college degrees, who have lost jobs because of cutbacks and downsizing. This has led to a large number of people losing their homes to foreclosure as they have not been able to afford the payments. Many of these same people when looking for new employment to replace the previous job are having difficulty getting entry level employment. No one is immune from the economic times in which we live. Even students of the teachings have to deal with these circumstances.

If you have experienced the loss of a job or home, intellectually you may be able to keep firm your understanding of the illusionary nature of adversity. However, paying bills with a limited money supply will "feel" nothing like an illusion. For the consistent practitioner of the teachings what you will notice during this time is that what you consider to be adversity is actually nothing more than "awareness" than actual adversity. This "awareness" was mentioned in the previous section but I will provide further detail on it now.

If you reflect on how your life was before you began to study the teachings of Shetaut Neter, in some ways it may appear that your life was better. You may have been working a better job so you may have had more money. With money relationships are easier to be in and maintain. Your mate may have also been working so in a combined way your income may have been substantially more.

But during this reflection time period ask yourself the following questions:

1. Were you "perpetually" happy?
2. Were you contributing anything substantive to the world?

During this reflection time do not fall prey to the "appearance" of how things were in the past as "appearances" can be deceiving. Aren't there many people who appear to be happy on the outside then you find out later on that they were actually miserable? Don't you see this quite often with the people who have fortune and fame? Aren't some of them consistently in the news for overdosing on the use of some type of drug or commit suicide? With them can't you see how appearances can be deceiving?

The problem is that many people and possibly you did not realize at the time that you were miserable when you lived in the world. This is because everyone else in the world felt the same way. Think about all of your family and friends. Have any of them experienced perpetual happiness for any prolonged period of time? Life in the world before your practice of the teachings of Shetaut Neter was a life where you did what the worldly people do. So it is difficult for anyone to be aware of how they truly feel when everyone else in their inner circle feels the same way. So it is easy to think during times of adversity that your previous life before you left the world was not that bad. Be careful during this time that you do not accept it as normal and do things against your conscience to deal with it (drinking, hanging out with friends etc.).

If channeled properly any adversity will allow you to realize that life before study of the teachings was not better than the one with the adversity. Even if you had more money or the relationship or things (cars, boats houses etc.), you weren't better off during that earlier time period for one big reason. During that time period you were beset with **IGNORANCE**. With ignorance you cannot know when you are miserable in one or many other ways. What you may feel like is adversity today is nothing more than the realization of what you were ignorant of previously. Before your study of the teachings what you did was suppress and bury your feelings of unhappiness. You chalked them up to being signs of a normal life. So there was nothing outwardly for you to deal with because it was all unconsciously bottled up inside. You "appeared" to be happy as life was better. But unconsciously you were creating the means for an earlier than had to be death (stress/heart attack), and ariu that would lead to your reincarnation.

While in the world, you did not realize it but you bought into the "ignorance is bliss" mentality. Mentally avoiding negative circumstances seems like it helps a person. I now know this is not the case. Ignorance keeps a person from ever having to accept responsibility for their actions. It is easy to blame someone else and continue doing things the same old way. However ignorance is not bliss. It comes with a cost.

The most important thing about adversity for you to realize is how we have created much of it all through our own actions. If you haven't yet, you soon will begin to understand that attachment to ideas and things that are not abiding is the cause of adversity. Consider this. The only reason to get upset when a person dies is because of attachment to the idea that the person should live forever. Although intellectually we know this cannot happen, we hold onto this desire. Since no life is permanent and abiding, when their eventual demise comes to an end, feelings of sadness are promised. Death has not caused suffering in this case. Attachment to the belief that life is permanent has.

If your life appears to be worse than it was prior to your studies of the teachings do not overlook the fact that your disappointed and frustrated moments are not the result of your circumstances. They were/are the result of the attachment you have to the idea that somehow "you" should not be in the present adverse situation. However, the reality is that life didn't promise anyone a rose garden. It is what it is. The more you accept it like this, the better off you will be in fulfilling the work you came into the world to do. Who knows, the current circumstance if dealt with thru detachment, may be providing lessons that will put you in a better position tomorrow. This same circumstance could also be showing you a weaker part of your personality. Weaknesses cannot be turned into strengths until realization of what they are first dawns.

"An Aspirant's Guide To Practicing The Egyptian Mysteries"

Attachment to ideas and things that are not abiding is the cause of suffering and adversity. Discover the areas in your life where you are attached, detach from it/them and you will eliminate adversity and suffering.

4. Judging Spiritual Progress

It is very difficult to keep yourself from judging your level of spiritual progress. Living in a microwave give me what I want right now world makes it difficult to be practice patience. Who doesn't want quantifiable results right now? Unfortunately judging spiritual advancement is not an area where we want to be making assessments in the traditional sense. Until the mind becomes purified, judging spiritual progress is difficult. It may also be harmful as expectation of higher advancement can cause frustration when the realization occurs that advancement has not progressed in the manner originally thought. Again the natural tendency for people is to judge their progress no matter what they are engaged in. This is an egotistical normal practice. However, spiritual practice should be monitored in a different way.

Becoming an excellent student of the teachings that lead to spiritual emancipation requires discipline and patience. It also requires daily practice and a deep desire to achieve a higher state in life. In some ways the practice itself separates the practitioner from the masses of people who live moment to moment not giving thought to the higher ideals in life.

Concern about the level of aspiration that a student represents is a never ending question and thought on the path. Judging the level of spiritual maturity and growth, if done, should be done with care and caution. It is similar to a young child who wants to be taller asking a family member everyday the following question. "Am I taller today?" Growth in height as well as growth in spiritual realization occurs in degrees. Although we do not realize it, every moment the body is growing in some way. So too, the level of spiritual growth occurs every moment for the student who continually practices the teachings.

One thing we can take solace in is the fact that the same practice you are engaged in RIGHT NOW was practiced in the SAME WAY by those great Sages and Saints and Priests and Priestesses of days gone by. Sages and Saints that we pay homage to with awe and admiration. Success for us is ASSURED as long as we practice the teachings in the integrated manner that they left for us. Given the fact that we have an authentic Preceptor, Teacher and Teaching, Nehast for us is assured.

When I want a concrete idea about my spiritual growth I sometimes will read different books published by Sema six months, one year or more after I originally read them. I am always amazed at how the exact same book and information gives me an entirely different perspective and insight today than it did when I originally read it. It is always a literal day vs. night difference in understanding. This is one way that I am able to determine that my growth is occurring when I choose to entertain the Ego (Set) in this way.

However, I no longer think about this question that much anymore. Granted the thought still does come up but I don't entertain it like I used to. I now KNOW I will achieve the goal in this lifetime and everything happening today is a movement in that direction. If I falter, I can speak with the preceptor or other students and do what's necessary to keep moving in the direction I have chosen. So I now have very little reason to worry about my spiritual progress. I TRUST the Path. I TRUST the Teaching. I TRUST the Preceptor, Teacher and my fellow Hemu/Asaru/Shemsu. Now my concentration can completely be on *"achieving a state of consciousness apart from bodily concerns." Egyptian Proverb.*

<u>Fallout from the Battle Within</u>

As your practice of the teachings intensifies, your desire for certain objects and activities in the world will dissipate. At some point you will no longer want to go out to parties. If single, you will no longer want to associate with people who drink or smoke. If married to a spouse who does not study the teachings, they may still go out to the party on weekends while you stay home. At some point you will not want to engage in long fruitless conversation filled with gossip. You may even lose the desire for shopping for clothes.

All of this will happen in time as you begin to discover that these types of activities are no longer exciting. Your study of the teachings will help you see a different aspect of these activities. The intermittent nature of the so called fun is what you will begin to see.

The desire to "hang out" and have "worldly fun" will decrease and stop as you decrease and stop receiving satisfaction from those activities. Or because of your practice of the teachings, you may develop a certain amount of detachment once you learn from them that negative activities are not righteous and not ultimately satisfying but entangling and lead to greater suffering. Here is where you will have to be careful because the receipt of this knowledge, even if you refrain from the activity, does not mean that you have become free from the desires --- because the desire has not been resolved and or the compelling energy may be too strong.

As your desire to engage in these types of activities wanes, your family and friends may start telling you that you have become boring. People who are tied to the world of time and space consistently seek activity within it to satisfy their desires. People often spend their entire life chasing desires of the world. Now that you have stopped this unachievable chase, you will be left with a lot of time on your hands. Once enlightened, this time is ok. But before reaching this state, you may have moments where you also might consider all of this free time to be boring. This may be the most difficult battle that you will face as it is easy to become frustrated. This is because you have not yet reached that state of perpetual contentment and peace while losing the lifestyle you had grown up knowing most of your life.

Most people do the worldly activities out of self-convincing (going along with the masses even though deep down they know it is not satisfying) that those are the way to get satisfaction and or happiness. If some dispassion is developed that may dampen the worldly desires and that may allow them space to delve into the teaching. If they are getting fulfilled by other activities, like the teaching, then the boredom will not be there –unless and until they reach a place where their progress reaches a plateau. Then higher teaching and or more intensity practice is required. Otherwise the spiritual practice becomes dull and ineffective. The desire is resolved through reinforcement of wisdom and higher experiences with the Divine (pleasure and fund from practicing the teachings, hanging out with other practitioners, etc. and the energy is resolved through redirection in a positive direction.

Until you become totally satisfied by activities such as the study and practice of the teachings and totally dissatisfied with worldly activities a sense of frustration may develop. This frustration may even heighten your desire to be free from the world quicker. But this heightened desire will not provide any solace in the moment. This frustration from being in the world but not yet above it is very difficult to deal with. At these moments you will feel like you are caught between

"An Aspirant's Guide To Practicing The Egyptian Mysteries"

two worlds. The fact of the matter is that this is true. At this time you will be caught between two worlds.

What Do I Do With All of This Time?

This is the time to be focused and increase the intensity of your Sheti practice. This can be done a couple of ways. One consideration is to reflect on something that you have always wanted to do and determine how that activity can be done in a way for the Divine. Ask yourself how you can turn this into selfless service. Then determine how the doing of this task can be done in a way that can supplement your income. Once this is determined, go about the task of doing this work. Don't quit your full time job. Do this new task during part time hours. Part time hours will be plentiful though as your non-activity in previous worldly activities will free up much time. Some of the things that you can do are teach meditation classes, do paintings or drawings of characters from the teachings, write books, plays or songs. You can also transcribe tapes from the Institute. There are many things you can do with this new time on your hands.

The best thing that you can do is any activities that you enjoy that will simultaneously expose you to longer periods of immersion into the teachings. The more activities that you engage in that center on Enlightenment, the easier it will be to let go of the world and attach onto the higher ideals in life.

Section III

Sheti Disciplines In Everyday Practice

Smai Tawi

"An Aspirant's Guide To Practicing The Egyptian Mysteries"

Section III-Introduction

What Can I Expect As I Practice the Teachings of Shetaut Neter on a daily basis?

Integral Sema Tawi (Yoga)

"The personality of every human being is somewhat different from every other. However, the Sages of Sema Tawi Yoga have identified four basic factors which are common to all human personalities. These factors are Emotions, Reason, Action and Will. This means that in order for a human being to evolve, all aspects of the personality must progress in an integral fashion. Therefore, four major forms of Sema disciplines have evolved. Each is specifically designed to promote a positive movement in one of the areas of the personality. The Sheti of Devotion was designed for the Emotions. The Sheti of Wisdom was designed for the Reasoning Intellectual aspect of the personality. The Sheti of Maat was designed for the action aspect of the personality that physically interacts in time and space. The Sheti of Meditation builds willpower and in the advanced stages leads the aspirant to higher planes of consciousness.

Thus, this Integral Sema Tawi Yoga approach is a way of spiritual living which transforms every aspect of the personality leaving no aspect of a human being behind."[6]

This section of the book will introduce for your consideration some of the "by-products" of the integrated practice of Shetaut Neter in your daily life. Each chapter in this section deals with the four specific disciplines of the practice. Then the section concludes with a discussion about the importance of the three- fold daily ritual, and detachment.

The "by-products" enumerated in the chapters are reflections of experiences I have had since I began my own practice of the teachings. Thru these shared experiences and the way in which they were handled, it is hoped that your own individualized practice may be a bit more manageable.

You have probably heard the saying "practice makes perfect!" This saying is now being modified by some who say that "perfect practice makes perfect!" It is

---

[6] From the Book "Initiation Into Egyptian Yoga and Neterian Spirituality by Dr. Muata Ashby.

probably safe to say that many believe that repetition of something is a key to mastery of that thing. When considering the importance of practice and repetition, one thing that gets lost in the consideration is the manner in which the daily practice affects the practitioner.

For example a person deciding to jog everyday for exercise may not initially think about the soreness their legs will experience. They may not consider the fact that their appetite is likely to increase. Additionally, they may have no clue that they may fall asleep earlier in the evening or at work. All of these "by-products" of the new practice, here with the example of jogging every day, will change the way a person lives their day to day to life.

Realization of the "by products" associated with the Integrated Sheti daily practice is the goal for this section of the book. An introduction to the effects of what you are now causing in your life by practice of the teachings may help you better manage your spiritual movement.

"An Aspirant's Guide To Practicing The Egyptian Mysteries"

NEBERDJER

The All Encompassing Divinity

"An Aspirant's Guide To Practicing The Egyptian Mysteries"

THE GODDESS MAAT AND MAAT PHILOSOPHY

Chapter 15

Righteousness in Action
Maat
Uashu

"Seek to perform your duties to your highest ability, This way your actions will be blameless."

"There are two roads traveled by humankind, those who seek To live MAAT and those who seek to satisfy their animal passions."

-Ancient Egyptian Proverbs

<u>*The Sheti of Maat cleanses/purifies the Active/Movement Aspect of the Personality!*</u>

To function in the world of time and space requires movement of our bodies. To move the body first requires movement of one's mind because the body acts in accordance with the thoughts generated from it. However, this relationship is reciprocal because the actions of the body leave impressions in the mind. Depending upon a person's beliefs about the action being undertaken, one of two types of conscious impressions will be left in the mind. An impression may be left in the mind creating desire for engagement of that same type of action at a later time. An impression may be left creating a desire to avoid that same type of action in the future.

Additionally, other impressions are left in the mind when the body is interacting in time and space. These impressions are subtle. They are unconscious. The belief that objects being interacted with through use of the body are "real" in a substantive way is one such impression. "Real" in this sense refers to the belief that these objects are abiding. Intellectually, we know that all objects no matter what form they present themselves as are coagulated energy in different forms. A tree for example is coagulated energy in the form of a tree. Although it may feel like it is "real" and abiding, we know that it is energy only. This tree is nothing more and nothing less than energy.

An impediment to achieving Nehast occurs anytime we interact with objects in time and space and forget that ALL objects are coagulated energy forms. This forgetfulness allows a person to "believe" that these objects are "real." This "belief" leaves an impression in the unconscious mind telling it that this thing I'm touching (a tree in this example) is separate and somehow different from me. This reinforces the belief that I am an individual among many other individuals. The belief that a person is an individual among other individuals is an impediment to obtaining Nehast.

The Sheti of Action is known as Uashu. To practice the Sheti of Uashu means that you will see and serve the Divine in all things that you interact with. It implies acting according to the teachings of mystical wisdom (Maat) throughout your normal day to day activities. This practice helps keep the mind occupied with thoughts which are uplifting to it. It has one see oneself as a vehicle of the Divine Self. Resultantly the mind begins to see the Divine working thru the performance of the actions. Not the ego/personality. One of the goals associated with its practice is to change the belief that "I am an individual among individuals" dynamic so that interactions with objects are done based upon the underlying reality of what these objects actually are. These objects are at their base energy. Therefore, interaction with objects in the world based upon the Sheti of Uashu has a person keep in mind to the extent possible that every interaction with anything is actually interaction with the Divine as it is the Divine Essence which makes up and is this energy. This is further complemented by the Sheti of Maat whereby one sees oneself as the Divine performing the action. Therefore, one's daily actions in the world do not distract from one's awareness of one's true Self.

Living life from this perspective transforms the mind in a positive way by cleansing it of the previous mistaken impressions just mentioned. This is important because the accumulation of all of these mistaken impressions creates a "veil" (aka, the Veil of Aset) over the mind preventing it from seeing the underlying oneness sustaining and giving rise to creation.

Unfortunately, the practice of interacting with objects in this higher way does not happen over night. Before this type of mindset can develop, the outer aspects of the personality must first be worked with and worked on. Living life everyday in accordance with the 42 Precepts of Maat purifies this outer aspect of the personality. Then the inner aspects can be worked on through the other Sheti practices which will be discussed further in this book.

To fully understand how this process is done, knowledge of the purification process is necessary. Additionally an understanding of the Goddess Maat, who she is and what she represents is also enjoined so that this aspect of the personality can be completely cleansed.

Forms of the Goddess Maat/Maati

Purification

Purification is a process designed to cleanse all aspects of the personality of beliefs (impressions) that prevent a person from having union with their Higher Conscious. This process allows a person to "awaken" to the higher reality called the SELF. This is called Nehast in our tradition and it means "awakening." Do not be mistaken and think that Enlightenment is something that a person has to obtain, achieve, or get. This type of thought assumes that Enlightenment is something that we presently do not have. In actuality, the Sheti purification practices will not "get" you anything. Everyone is already Enlightened as it is the basis of our essential nature. Unfortunately we have forgotten about this nature and no longer have "realization" of it. This is what we "awaken" to. It is as if the "veil" spoken of previously has been placed over our ability to experience this higher aspect of our being. The purification process cleanses the "veil" so that we can see thru it with our awakened "eye of intuition" and become conscious of our higher essential nature.

The Sages and Saints of Ancient Kamit have given us a guide to use in our daily life that leads the purification process. The guide is known as the 42 Precepts of Maat. In the book, "The Wisdom of Maati," by Dr. Muata Ashby on page 76 the following was stated when the question, "Who is Maat?," was asked.

"Maat is a philosophy, a spiritual symbol as well as a

cosmic energy or force which pervades the entire universe. She is the symbolic embodiment of world order, justice, Righteousness, correctness, harmony and peace. She is also known by her headdress composed of a feather of truth. She is a form of the Goddess Aset, who represents wisdom and spiritual awakening through balance and equanimity."

In the ancient Kamitic system of spirituality, the Goddess Maat stood for the order of Creation itself. When the universe was created, order replaced chaos. Therefore Creation itself is Maat. When a person lives their life according to the principles of Maat, they are bringing their life into harmony and balance with the harmony and balance of Creation itself.

The Goddess Maat is also the daughter of Ra/God. In many reliefs in the temples of Kemet, you will see Goddess Maat opening the way for her father Ra as he travels the ocean of consciousness. On a spiritual level these reliefs mean that before we can gain full spiritual illumination (realization of our connection to the Divine), we must first be balanced in every aspect of our life (Practice Maat). This also means that order and purification in a person's life is necessary before spiritual liberation can occur. One comes before the other. Therefore  purification through the practice of Maat brings order to your life which allows illumination to occur. Without the first, you do not receive the second.

There are 42 precepts or injunctions which you should be able to answer affirmatively at the end of each day. The goal is to live your daily life in such a way that you can answer these questions honestly. This is the first thing that you should begin doing as of this moment. Begin living your life in accordance with these precepts on a daily basis.

42 Precepts of Maat[7]

The 42 Precepts of Maat have been called "wisdom in action" by Dr. Muata Ashby. Without a steady and consistent practice of these precepts, the ability to

---

[7] From the Book, Shetaut Neter Daily Chant, Songbook, Meditation and Devotional Worship Manual By Muata Ashby 2003

understand the subtle and higher aspects of the teachings will not be able to occur. Therefore Enlightenment will occur slowly or not at all.

1. "I have not done iniquity." Variant: Acting with falsehood.
2. "I have not robbed with violence."
3. "I have not done violence to anyone or anything." Variant: Rapacious-taking by force; plundering.
4. "I have not committed theft." Variant: Coveted.
5. "I have not murdered man or woman." Variant: Or ordered someone else to commit murder.
6. "I have not defrauded offerings." Variant: or destroyed food supplies or increased or decreased the measures to profit.
7. "I have not acted deceitfully." Variant: I have not acted with crookedness.
8. "I have not robbed the things that belong to God."
9. "I have told no lies."
10. "I have not snatched away food."
11. "I have not uttered evil words. Variant: I have not allowed myself to become sullen, to sulk or become depressed.
12. "I have attacked no one."
13. "I have not slaughtered the cattle that are set apart for the Gods." Variant: I have not slaughtered the sacred bull-(Apis)
14. "I have not eaten my heart" (overcome with anguish and distraught). Variant: I have not committed perjury.
15. "I have not laid waste the ploughed lands."
16. "I have not been an eavesdropper or pried into matters to make mischief."
17. "I have not spoken against anyone." Variant: I have not babbled, gossiped.
18. "I have not allowed myself to become angry without cause."
19. "I have not committed adultery." Variant: I have not committed homosexuality.
20. "I have not committed any sin against my own purity."
21. "I have not violated sacred times and seasons."
22. "I have not done that which is abominable."
23. "I have uttered fiery words. I have not been a man or woman of anger."
24. "I have not stopped my ears listening to the words of right and wrong (Maat)."
25. "I have not stirred up strife (disturbance)." "I have not caused terror." "I have not struck fear into any man."
26. "I have not caused any one to weep." Variant: I have not hoodwinked.
27. "I have not lusted or committed fornication nor have I lain with others of my same sex." Variant: I have not molested children.

28. "I have not avenged myself." <u>Variant: I have not cultivated resentment.</u>
29. "I have not worked grief, I have not abused anyone." <u>Variant: I have not cultivated a quarrelsome nature.</u>
30. "I have not acted insolently or with violence."
31. "I have not judged hastily." <u>Variant: I have not been impatient.</u>
32. "I have not transgressed or angered God."
33. "I have not multiplied my speech overmuch. (talk too much)."
34. "I have not done harm or evil. <u>Variant: I have not thought evil.</u>
35. "I have not worked treason or curses on the King."
36. "I have never befouled the water." <u>Variant: I have not held back the water from flowing in its season.</u>
37. "I have not spoken scornfully." <u>Variant: I have not yelled unnecessarily or raised my voice.</u>
38. "I have not cursed the God."
39. "I have not behaved with arrogance." <u>Variant: I have not been boastful.</u>
40. "I have not been overwhelmingly proud or sought for distinctions for myself."
41. "I have never magnified my condition beyond what was fitting or increased my wealth, except with such things as are (justly) mine own possessions by means of Maat." <u>Variant: I have not disputed over possessions except when they concern my own rightful possessions. Variant: I have not desired more than what is rightfully mine.</u>
42. "I have never thought evil (blasphemed) or slighted the God in my native town."

<u>How Do I Practice Maat In Everyday Life?</u>

You may be thinking that practicing forty two injunctions everyday seems to be a bit much. Given people's inability to practice ten (The Ten Commandments), how in the world can a person practice forty two everyday? The answer to that question is simple. Don't practice them. It is much easier to live them than to practice them.

With reflection you will notice that many things you have to practice quickly become work. There are a few people who enjoy what they practice. For most people, anything perceived as work quickly becomes a chore to do. Unless the person is highly disciplined, it will be a short time before their practice ends. Understanding this process will help you move beyond it.

"An Aspirant's Guide To Practicing The Egyptian Mysteries"

One thing that works well in being able to "live" the Precepts is to do the following. Each night before you go to bed, read the 42 Precepts above out loud. Nothing more, nothing less. In a short matter of time, you will find yourself becoming aware of situations where you are not acting in accordance with one of the precepts. For example gossiping which you may have done previously without any awareness of doing it, will now be replaced with conscious awareness of what you are doing. Although the new consciousness will not immediately stop you from gossiping, the newfound awareness of what you are doing will allow you to cut the conversation to a minimum. In a short matter of time, this new awareness will grow and will be remembered right before you begin to start gossiping. Then it will be easy to refrain from engaging in the conduct. Once you stop gossiping in general, it will be much easier to stop gossiping altogether. Then it will also be easier to not entertain this dialogue from others.

The simple practice of reading the precepts before you go to bed each night will raise your conscious awareness about each one. This is better than having to practice the precepts everyday. Who wants 42 more things to remember to do every day? This is important because one of the by-products of living the 42 Precepts of Maat in everyday life is for it to become something to do (work). This by-product can be avoided by living the precepts instead of practicing them.

Stress

Have you ever heard the term "keep your conscience clear?" I believe that living life in harmony with the precepts of Maat gave rise to the saying "keep your conscience clear."

If you review the precepts above you will notice that all of them, if done, keep a person's conscience clear. A clear conscience can be distinguished from an unclear one. An unclear conscience is filled with worry, and many concerns. Conversely a clear conscience allows a person to have a life free from worry and those same concerns. Another name for worry and many concerns is stress.

In today's society, there does not seem to be a clear idea of what stress is. People just know that they are stressed out but they really don't why. Although people know the factors that cause stress, working too much, worry, anxiety and more, they are not clear on what stress actually is. Stress is a direct reflection of having a conscience that is not clear. An unclear conscience is "heavy" as opposed to "light." As you read other books published by the Sema Institute of Yoga or other works from those people helping the populace achieve spiritual liberation,

"An Aspirant's Guide To Practicing The Egyptian Mysteries"

you will find that the phrase "mental agitation" is often used. Often this term is used to describe a barrier to spiritual enlightenment. This "agitation" prevents the mind and conscience from being clear. Without a "clear and light" mind, higher spiritual realization is not possible.

A friend of mine recently told me that she typically lives a life in which her mind is usually "light." By this she meant that she is usually free from worry. However, when dealing with one of her children and the significant people in her life, she looses the "light" mind and gets "weighed" down based upon issues that they have. My friend did not realize the significance of what she said regarding her mind being "light" at times and "weighed down" at others.

The underlying cause of stress for a person is mental agitation. This agitation is the sum total of all of the things going on in a person's mind that cause worry or concern. Surprisingly mental agitation is also caused by so-called happy feelings. Mental agitation acts like a weight in our minds. Literally it "weighs our minds down." We describe the manifestation of this process as stress. For example, if you steal or do violence to others or do anything wrong, your conscience will not be clear. Although no one else may know what happened, deep down inside you will know and this knowledge will cause your mind to be agitated. If you lie and gossip, deep down inside the same thing will happen. You will know that you did something wrong. This too will cause agitation in your mind. Individually all of these wrongful actions may not appear to amount to much. But when you add them up collectively, you find a person with a "weighed down" mind. This mind is weighed down because their conscience is "full" of all the things a person knows they should not have done. This type of conscience cannot be clear.

A "weighed down" mind is also created when so called "happy moments" are experienced in life. Mental agitation is caused anytime the mind desires and seeks for something occurring outside of itself. Happy moments are never abiding. Therefore, until the next "happy" moment comes, an underlying desire to have another happy moment will create a sense of frustration, longing, and disappointment until the next "happy" moment arrives. This is mental agitation and can be noticed as such when you hear a person say things such as, "I deserve better than this!" Unfortunately people don't realize that the time between the next "happy moment" lasts far longer than the experience of the "happy moment" itself. The only constant in this "happy moment" example is the fact that the mind is agitated "both" while waiting for the next happy moment and while experiencing it. Even in this case, the mind is still "weighed down," albeit this time because of frustration masquerading as happiness. Thus the true source of mental agitation is ignorance of Self.

In either case this person is carrying a lot of mental agitation. Unfortunately, many of us do not realize that we are carrying such a heavy mental load. We are so accustomed to living our lives in this way that we don't realize how heavy these loads are. Those born in the society of the Western world who adopted that system of cultural values and beliefs consider it quite normal to have a mind that is "weighed down"/agitated. In a way this person is stuck. Since they don't know that this process is mentally doing them harm, they have no reason to stop it. Also because they believe this is a normal way of being, they don't seek to find a better way of living. If someone tries to show them a better way to exist, they will dismiss it because they believe the person is somehow deluding themselves. Resultantly little if anything is done in this society to show people how to take the "weight off" their minds. "Weighed down"/agitated minds are the norm.

If you take time and reflect on each of the 42 Precepts of Maat, you will find that the implementation of each one in your life will keep your conscience clear in that specific area. For ease of implementation, read them once each day, preferably before you retire for the evening. I read these to my 12 year old daughter on an intermittent basis. When she has rough periods in her life, she will remind me to read them to her. This is her way of strengthening her conscience as she deals with the challenges of life from a 12 year old point of view. Simply reading them awakens your consciousness in that area when it is presented to you in the course of your daily life. This is how I have been able to make the precepts a part of my life without having to work at it. The more you do this, the more the precepts will become a part of you. As this happens, your mind will become "light" as my friend put it. This is because this will reduce the underlying cause of stress in your life as it will reduce mental agitation. This is righteousness in action and this paves the way to your attainment of Nehast. It is this process that will bring you into harmony and balance with creation itself. It is this process that "opens the way" to spiritual enlightenment. It is also this process that purifies the active movement aspect of the personality.

Discernment and Discriminative Knowledge of What is Real and What is Not Real.

Chapter 16

Wisdom in Practice
Rekh

*"Hear the words of prudence, give heed unto her counsels,
And store them in thine heart; her maxims are universal,
And all the virtues lean upon her; she is the guide
And the mistress of human life."*

-Ancient Egyptian Proverb

<u>*The Sheti of Wisdom purifies the Intellect.*</u>

By far the most difficult aspect of practicing the teachings for me was the wisdom practice. The wisdom practice is designed to purify the intellect of the personality. It requires listening to the teachings which is also the same as studying and reading them. The Wisdom practice was not difficult because of problems I had reading or understanding. As a former attorney by trade, reading large amounts of information was something that I was used to. Reading was actually something that I enjoyed quite a bit. What was difficult for me was what I was supposed to do with the information once I read it. My intellect that I was supposed to be purifying was getting in the way of gaining the higher understanding of what the teachings were designed to impart. Throughout many of the first few years of practicing Shetaut Neter, and even sometimes today, a subtle form of arrogance prevented me from gaining all that I could have from a text.

Aset

People with intellectual acuity sometimes have an underlying belief that they can achieve mastery over subjects by simply reading them. Society does not help matters as it acts with awe towards those people who can memorize and/or recite large amounts of information. This is what happened to me. After so many of years of being looked at as intelligent because of my profession, it was difficult for me to <u>fully</u> accept the guidance of Goddess Aset as taught in her Temple. This is the arrogance, the internal belief that once I read something I understood it.

147

Goddess Aset is the Goddess of Wisdom. Her teachings, if practiced properly bestow, "intuitional" knowledge of the Divine Self that is Nehast. The teachings espoused in her Temple were designed to raise the consciousness of the person through their intellect. This was done through the following process:

1) Listening to the Teachings;
2) Reflection on those Teachings; and then
3) Meditation on those Teachings.

I had no problem with number one which is listening to the teachings. I had no problem with number three, meditation on the teachings. I had big problems with number two, reflection on those teachings, and consequently unknowingly did not derive maximum benefit with meditation on them. It has been in the later years of my practice that I have realized that what I once considered as my strength (my intellect) was actually one of my biggest weaknesses. The reasons why this was so will become clear shortly.

1. Listening to the Teachings

It is enjoined that an Aspirant listen to and study those teachings that will purify particular aspects of the personality. Listening is done by actually listening to the teachings imparted by a Spiritual Preceptor live. Listening can also be done by listening to a taped recording of teachings imparted by a preceptor, and/or reading materials produced by the Sages of yesterday or today. The most important wisdom information to listen to and/or read in our tradition comes from the following:

a) Tradition of Ra;
b) Tradition of Ptah;
c) Tradition of Amun;
d) Tradition of Asar;
e) The Goddess Path or Tradition; and
f) The Tradition of Aton.

All of these traditions contain within them, myths and rituals that purify the personality. The myths especially are important to listen to and reflect on. They serve as a bridge between us and the Divine. In our current state, we perceive reality through senses which are not accurate. Therefore our sense of reality is skewed. Myths provide the mind with something to hold onto until it is able to let go of its illusionary ideas of what reality is.

2. Reflection on the Teachings

What does it mean to reflect on the Teachings once you have listened to them? In the teachings of the Temple of Aset, a devotee of Aset is described as *"one who ponders over sacred matters and seeks therein for hidden truth."* Plutarch, the famous Greek philosopher, was a student of the Temple of Aset. He wrote the following about what it means to reflect on the teachings.

"He alone is a true servant or follower of this goddess who, after has heard, and has been made acquainted in a proper manner (initiated into the philosophy) with the history of the actions of these gods, searches into the hidden truths which lie concealed under them, and examines the whole by the dictates of reason and philosophy."

Reflection is the process of pondering or thinking about what was listened to in a deep way to discover the underlying lesson being imparted. It also allows the teachings to become applicable and effective in one's practical life. It is a process which takes time. It is a process which requires a certain skill. Reflection is a process that I did not do.

I had a difficult time with reflection because I believed that reading was reflecting. I confused reflection with reading comprehension. As long as I understood what was going on in the myth, I must have been doing okay. This mistaken belief was what made this part of the practice so difficult. Not knowing that my understanding of what reflection of was off. How can a person ask for assistance when they don't think they need it?

3. Meditation on the Teachings

Sebai Muata Ashby defines meditation as "a process of directing your attention inward to discover your higher nature or Self." More on meditation will be discussed in the later chapter devoted to it. But in the context of the Wisdom Teachings brought forth in the Temple of Aset, meditation was the step taken <u>after</u> the reflection process had occurred.

Although I had no problem meditating on the teachings which I had listened to, my inability to reflect created a gap in my ability to fully absorb the teachings. Reflection done in a concentrated way leads to a meditative state itself.

Concentration and focus on any one thing does that. Reflection turns the attention of the listened material inwards. This practice purifies the subconscious aspect of our being. This is also known as our astral body. The mind is in this body. Unfortunately our minds interpret information it receives from our senses in the only way it is accustomed to. Therefore its perceptions are skewed. Reflection allows our mind to expand and begin interpreting the data received by our senses in a different way. Information received by the mind through the reflection process is not skewed and is based upon the ultimate truth. This is a good thing. The more this is done, the more purified and expansive our minds become. As this occurs, the subtle wisdom being imparted through the teachings is realized. Meditation on those teachings which have now been reflected on as the final step then produces such a deep absorption that enlightened impressions are left in the unconscious mind (casual body). These impressions over time lead to "intuition." This is how Goddess Aset through her wisdom bestows intuitional knowledge on the aspirant.

Conclusion

Keep in mind that the Goddess Aset represents the wisdom and devotional love inherent in every person. Although she is a deity, for purposes of higher awareness she and the other Gods and Goddess represent cosmic forces and specific aspects of the individual person. Based upon the myths where Aset is a part, you find that she has "inner" access to the Divine. Therefore she represents the aspect of each person who too already has this access. The problem for the individual is that they have forgotten about this. The process of reflection on the topic being studied, (myth, proverb, text ect.) is the key element which allows "intuitional knowledge" to come forth. Intuitional knowledge is the link that allows remembering of the "inner" access to the Divine that has been forgotten.

To this day I sometimes still have to fight my tendency of putting my wisdom texts down immediately after I have read them. I still have to be aware of my habit of moving on to the next thing as soon as I finish the one I am currently doing. (Making a phone call or getting something to eat for example) However, this is the process that has been enjoined that allows for the development of "intuitional" knowledge about the Divine.

Instead I now focus on spending a minimum of a half hour reflecting on material I have listened to or read after its completion. The amount of time depends upon the amount of material I have read. Only after I have done this reflection will I meditate on them. Sometimes I will go for a walk and "think" about the material. If it's a myth, I reflect on the characters and see myself as the character who wins in the end. I ponder about what the Sages were attempting to convey on all levels when they composed the writings. (Conscious, subconscious, and unconscious) Other times I may go sit by the pool at my apartment complex and allow only thoughts about the teachings to cross my mind.

After all of this is done, then I smile and congratulate myself for practicing the teachings the way they were designed to be studied. I smile and realize that through this practice, my spiritual awareness has just grown by another degree!

"An Aspirant's Guide To Practicing The Egyptian Mysteries"

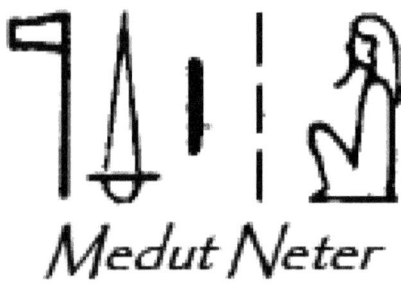

Medut Neter
"Speech (words) of the Divinity"

Chapter 17

Devotion in Practice
Ushet

"Oh behold with thine eye God's plans. Devote thyself To adore God's name. It is God who giveth Souls to Millions of forms, and God magnifyeth Whosoever magnifyeth God."

-Ancient Egyptian Proverb

The Sheti of Devotion purifies the Emotional aspect of the personality.

When I began my study of Shetaut Neter, I thought that the Devotional Path was the most in line with my personality make-up. Resultantly I studied the books about this path and acted in accordance with its practices. Intellectually it seemed like a rather easy practice. First, shift the attention and focus of your Love and emotional feelings for all people and things to the Divine/God. Then, see the underlying essence of the Divine/God in all people and things instead of seeing their outer appearance. "What's so difficult about that?" I thought. As I have grown in my practice of the overall teachings of Shetaut Neter, what I once considered as easy (the Devotional Path), has proven to be just as difficult for me as reflection on the teachings was/is.

This difficulty arose because of my acceptance of the definition of what love is in our society. Additionally, it arose because of the role I gave/give emotions in my everyday life. As it relates to love, what is considered to be Love in western societal cultures is anything but loving. It is actually a very selfish and self-centered practice, as it relates to emotions and emotional states. Societal customs promote the allowance of these as master over the personality instead of being servants to it.

So when Dr. Muata Ashby (Sebai Maa) shared the following words with me about what the Sheti practice of Devotion is, my ability to grasp fully the depth of what was being imparted escaped me.

"This path is like falling in love with a person, which in a way is irrational, but instead falling in love with a form of the Divine, a form that allows one's feelings to open up and experience the deeper nature of that Divine with feelings. As in love with a person, one finds out about them, learning about them by spending time with them. An aspirant spends time through study of a myth and practice of the rituals related to the myth. Through ritual there is the touching, the holding of the symbols of the divine lover and caressing the images and treasuring of their words and deeds, that is, their teaching, and then there are the little things that lovers do for each other, the bringing of gifts (offerings), the dressing up, the washing of the object of love, the calling of the beloved's name and the Divine responds with comforting and unconditional acceptance of the aspirant and the opening up of inner space of peace and contentment.

There is the learning about the little things that the lover does, likes and feels and thinks about and the desire to please the lover more than oneself. That, by living with that Divine, and seeing the world with Her as She sees it, and going through the same struggle with Him as He goes through it, a wider and magnanimous perspective arises in the heart, and feeling with them, crying with them through the struggle of their ordeal, which is also our ordeal, and then finally being triumphant with them and all the things that go with supporting the loved one and being supported by them so a bond that transcends sorrows and failures and gains and losses and life and death is created.

Then there is the Tantric aspect of Divine Love, the merging, the making love and the after glow of lovemaking with the Divine that unlike lovemaking in the world, here becomes perennial. And then there is the offspring of that lovemaking, the child of light that grows in the heart as the Divine impregnates one with the spirit of self-knowledge, this is the mysticism.

The neophyte grows into the mature initiate and then the master, the victor over the forces of hate and greed that is one's ego and selfish desires. And that love, being victorious over egoism, now also is universal and not just reserved for the Divine form, for that being is in reality a representation of all there is and one's love has expanded one's feeling capacity to encompass all that is. And so there is ecstasy and satisfaction that no earthly way of loving or love for material things can provide, and there is the pleasure of incomparable bliss of knowing the Divine with intellect but also with heart so that understanding and feeling blend into a totality of knowing and awakening such terms like satisfaction, contentment and peace are apt but still incomplete words to describe the experience of such a one who has succeeded on this path.

Having realized that love is born of the realization of one's own magnanimousness, one's own glory, which is shared with all and manifests as all and having realized that one is beautiful, worthy and detached, then one can see others and the environment as images of the Divine and share that same love with them by doing good to and for them as service, but really as one's advanced expression of love, which is caring, and sharing with them as one with them even if they do not understand or appreciate it."
-Dr. Muata Ashby
July 20, 2007

Upon my first few readings of these words, I was not able to fully grasp what was being imparted. Although intellectually I understood them, I couldn't relate to them because of where I was mentally regarding my personal thoughts of what love and emotions are.

It has been three years since I first read these words. Today for the first time I think I have a sliver of an idea of what Sebai Maa was conveying. Devotional Love was not as easily practiced by me because I didn't understand the depth of what it really meant/means.

This should not be surprising given the concept of love that surrounds those who live in a world governed by those who practice the western societal cultural standards and norms. Consider the following about love in our society. Generally speaking, people tend to love those people or things that satisfy their wants and needs. When wants and needs are satisfied by a person, love flows in an endless way. However, love immediately stops when those same wants and needs stop being satisfied and fulfilled by that same person. To quote Janet Jackson, it is a "what have you done for me lately?" practice. Although it feels very good while in the midst of it, love practiced in this way is very cold and mean. This is because love like this is conditional.

Love like this is not what Dr. Ashby was referring to above. Love as described by Sebai Maa is the highest form of Love because it is unconditional. This is one of the ways I found the Devotional practice to be difficult. I did not know what unconditional anything was let alone unconditional love. The "what have you done for me lately" type of love was the only reference point I had about what love was/is. Not surprisingly, fully grasping what was being imparted above was not an easy thing to do.

Another reason that I found the Devotional practice to be difficult was because of the variety of ways that love is expressed in society. In my experiences the people I have grown up with and spent significant time with, all grew up in households that had love "practices" that differed from mine. Therefore, familial patterns of what love is and how it is expressed differed in each household. These divergent practices about the definition and expression of what love is has created an overall state where you wind up with what one book refers to today, as "several love languages."

So there is no consistency for what love is considered to be and how it is supposed to "practiced or expressed." These differences made it difficult for me to fully understand the teachings as it relates to this area of the Sheti practice.

For me, I grew up in an environment where the love that was practiced was done from a distance. Although people could be in the same room or house, we did not talk much. When we did talk it was more about general things. Rarely did I feel comfortable expressing inner life personal feelings and thoughts. Without that comfort, I grew older and older expressing less and less, until one day I had no thoughts about expressing these types of feelings. Additionally, in relationships with others, I did not see the need for anyone to express this to me. Some describe this as the emotional aspect of love. This emotional aspect of love is something that I did not experience as I grew up.

What I considered to be love had little to do with an emotional state. Except for those moments when I met a new girlfriend and experienced the "puppy dog love" initial reaction, I don't ever recall experiencing an emotional loving state with anyone or with anything. For me love was more a reflection of support, stability, reliability, and trust. There was nothing touchy or feely about it. This limited idea about love ended up hindering my practice of the Devotional Path of Yoga/Shetaut Neter. One thing that you may want to consider is the following as you live a spiritual life. No matter what type or style of love you grew up believing in, inherently it too was/is limited. Why? Because loving styles in many cultures due to egoism are conditional.

Equating the satisfaction of wants and needs as love is conditional for a couple of reasons. First because wants and needs change. They never stay the same. The wants and needs I have as a 47 year old man is much different than those I had when I was 17, 27 or 37. They will again be different in ten years when I am 57 and so on.

Next, this practice of love is conditional because these wants and needs will not be satisfied by another person forever. Although they may be satisfied for short intervals of time, months or a few years, as people grow and evolve, their continued satisfaction of these specific wants and needs will stop, not because their love for that person stops, but because as the person grows and evolves, their expression of love for that person will grow and evolve as well.

The Path of Devotional Love recognizes the conditional nature of the love practiced by many today. Thru its practices, the aspirant is able to discover "the unconditional practice of love." This practice purifies the emotional aspect of the personality and was described by Sebai Maa in the excerpt above, and also in his book "The Path of Divine Love: Blooming Lotus of Divine Love." The Divine Love book provides further elucidation on this practice and describes it "as a movement in which the emotions of the person are purified and directed towards the Divine Self."[8]

Therefore, no matter what love style, love language or inclination that a person has developed, the Sheti of Devotion will purify the emotional aspect of that personality. This is important to realize, as quite often what is believed to be loved by a person, someone or something, it is actually not love for that someone or something. It is actually love for the "underlying essence" manifesting as that particular someone or something. The "underlying essence" of any thing is the Divine/God and it's a reflection of that Divine spark within the person or objects that catches our attention, but then if the mind does not understand this or knows better, it attributes the positive feeling of that Divine Spark to the physical object or person rather than the Divine.

The manifestation of what is called Love occurs because a person is better able to "see" the underlying Essence, (the Divine) in that someone or something better than they can see it in others or things. Resultantly the Sheti of Devotion is a movement which moves the mind towards the realization of what about the object is actually being desired. This path allows the practitioner to realize that it is the "underlying essence" of that someone or something which is the Divine/God!

---

[8] "The Path of Divine Love: Blooming Lotus of Divine Love" by Dr. Muata Ashby pg. 65

In the Divine Love book, Sebai Maa provides detailed instruction on "how" to practice Devotion in the every day setting of the world. In it he states that "Devotional Yoga has developed into a program which involves following the integrated aspects of practices whose purpose is to lead the aspirant to develop a mental process which is one pointedly directing all thoughts and emotions towards the Divine. These practices are:

1. Listening to the Teachings;
2. Singing, Chanting and Divine Music,
3. Service;
4. Ritual Worship;
5. The Supreme Offering; and
6. Meditation."[9]

The process is designed to have an aspirant live their life in such a way that they spiritualize every moment of it. Essentially, the Path of Devotion allows a person to see the Divine in all things at all times and also see the Divine in others. This practice purifies the emotional aspect of the personality. Devotion, when practiced in the six ways as expressed daily, allows a person to spiritualize every moment of their life. The continued spiritualization practice over time allows a person to literally be able to "see" the Divine Essence/Neter as the underlying essence in all things. This is the ultimate truth of existence and will be experienced by those who purify every aspect of their personality thru the integrated practice of the teachings.

The reality is that there is no individuality of anything. Everything that exists is a manifestation of the ONE Essence known by many cultures with different names: Allah, Buddha, Consciousness, Elohim, and God the Father, Jesus, Krishna, Nirvana, etc. In our tradition this is known as the Self, Divine, or Neberjder.

1. <u>Listening to the Teachings</u>

Listening to the Teachings, as discussed in the previous chapter, involves the process of listening to or reading wisdom teachings. The process also involves having an open mind when this interaction is occurring. At its depth, it means listening to these words with the desire to understand the underlying meaning in them. The wisdom teachings have been written in such a way that they can appeal to the subtle aspect of a person. Listening to understand the subtle lessons being

---

[9] "Id. At pgs 118-140."

given by asking what is the deeper meaning being imparted is the desired goal. This is the proper way to listen to them.

2. Singing, Chanting and Divine Music

Singing, Chanting and Divine Music take the mind to higher consciousness levels as music has the ability to induce a mind that is *lucid*. A *lucid* mind is a mind that is free from being bombarded with various egoistic thoughts and imaginations that run rampant in the typical mind of a person. It is a controlled mind. A lucid mind is peaceful because it is able to be still. The stillness allows this mind to see life in a deeper way. The lucid mind is a mind filled with pure thoughts and desires which do not obstruct vision of the higher Self but rather which flows from the higher Self.

This type of mind differs from the *agitated* and *dull* types of mind that also exist. The *agitated* mind is the type of mind that most people have. It is characterized by moments in which it is always moving from one egoistic thought to the next in an uncontrolled way. Without rhyme or reason, this mind races from one thing to the next. Although this type of mind does have intermittent moments of lucidity, its tendency is on the side of constant movement. The agitated mind moves even when a person is asleep. This mind during sleep still moves/dreams about what it didn't get done the previous day and/or what still needs to be done the following one.

The *dull* mind is a mind beset with depression, anguish, hatred and unrest in varying degrees. People with dull minds perform actions that are detrimental to spiritual, mental and or physical health. They stay on jobs that cause them illness. They stay with marital partners that are unfaithful or unrighteous or are themselves unfaithful to their partners. They maintain activities injurious to their health like smoking or using drugs and accept religious burdens/teachings that they know are un-spiritual.[10]

Singing and/or chanting hekau or words of power and listening to Divine music quiets and stills the agitated and dull minds. These activities calm both types of minds and allow them to experience moments of lucidity by allowing the mind to flow to the source of peace. The more moments of lucidity experienced by the mind, the more the mind will "remember" the lucid state. These experiences leave positive impressions in the mind. The more this state is experienced, the more the

---

[10] From the book Kemetic Diet, by Dr. Muata Ashby.

mind will gravitate towards actions that will lead it back to this state. Additionally, as this state is achieved on more and more occasions, the mind will then be free to experience higher realms of consciousness.

Singing, chanting and listening to Divine music are very important activities that help still the mind which allows it to "see" the "underlying essence" which supports and gives rise to all of Creation.

3. <u>Service to the Divine</u>

Service to the Divine, also known as selfless service, is expressed as service to humanity. These are actions done by a person for the betterment of all people with no thought or desire for something in return. Service to humanity is actually service to the Divine as all things in creation are manifestations of the Divine Self. When this practice is done, the ego of the person is effaced. When you do actions for the overall good of humanity instead of for the purpose of individual self-gratification, your ego will become sublimated.

Oftentimes when people engage in service to others, there is a desire to receive something from those that have benefited from the service. Service in this way is not selfless. It can't be, because the action is being done to receive something. That something could be something big like a financial payment, or as small as someone saying thank you. It is safe to say that most of us perform actions with an unconscious expectation that we will be rewarded. The reward may be big or small, but it is there.

Be careful because few realize that this thinking is actually binding as this way of thinking allows your emotional state to be dictated by others. For example, as soon as I expect to derive a sense of satisfaction or pleasure from someone thanking me for a good deed that I may do, I may be easily disappointed. This is because not all people will think my action was worthy of a thank you. Some will, but others won't. Many will not thank me for the action that was done and there is nothing I can do about it. When a thank you does not come, this is when many people who are unaware get upset or even angry at what they will now consider as a lack of appreciation.

The important point to keep in mind is this. Another person's "reaction" to an action from you cannot be controlled. You are only capable of controlling one thing. The "original action" itself!

Selfless service, when practiced is the process of doing certain types of actions for the "internal" purification that comes as a result of doing the action itself. The response of others is not looked for to derive a sense of satisfaction or pleasure.

The highest form of Selfless Service for a Shemsu (follower of the Divine) is service done to help the Preceptor disseminate the Teachings. As the Preceptor, thru his or her works is creating the means by which humanity will be able to hasten its movement in consciousness; this service is the ultimate service to the Divine. This service has an additional benefit. It allows the person engaged in the service the opportunity to find favor with the Preceptor. This is a great thing as the subtle aspect of the teachings can only be learned by one who has the subtle understanding of what the teachings have been designed to impart.

Further, whereas it may not be so easy to be able to see the Divine in others you are serving, due to the spiritual bond and deep regard if not affection for the Preceptor, when performing even the most mundane of tasks, you will find that you are able to feel the Divine Self is working through your performing the tasks (Yoga of Right Action and Selfless Service) and that you are serving the Divine in others. {Here the "others" is the Preceptor [Devotional Yoga]}.

Ritual Worship

To practice Ritual Worship, it must be understood that the unpurified mind is not yet ready to "experience" the higher nature or "Self" as this experience is transcendental. Until the mind is purified, the mind must be given a concrete form to focus its attention on. This makes sense as concrete forms of imagery is the only thing a mind beset with ignorance is used to being aware of anyway. Deity images are chosen as a means of worship because they represent concrete aspects of the Divine.

Every Kamitan Temple has a tutelary deity. The tutelary symbol is a focal point for the aspirations, reflections and meditations of a spiritual aspirant. When we refer to the Temple of Asar or the Temple of Heru, we are speaking of the deity of the Temple; it means that particular Temple focuses on that particular divinity, not to the exclusion of others, but rather as a highlight. Each deity offers some unique mode of insight into the teachings and leads to higher self-knowledge. The tutelary deity serves as the main icon of worship and shapes the focus of the energies of the mind of the aspirant through reflection and meditation and the cosmic energy that the Temple collects and manipulates. In the early stages of practice of religion the mind needs an object of worship. The tutelary icons satisfy this need.

Praises, songs and forms of expression are devoted to this image with the firm understanding that the image represents an aspect of the Divine. The image is NEVER considered to be the "only" God itself. Actually it is possible to consider an image as a manifestation of the Divine. In fact, all matter is an expression of the Divine so why not the image also? The problem is considering that image as THE expression and no others exist. That is idolatry. The person utilizing a deity as a means of worship has a concrete aspect of the Divine to focus their mind on. The concentrated focus on the concrete aspect as reflected in the image eventually gives way to the transcendental nature of the Divine itself. This practice "opens the way" to experience of the transcendental nature of the Divine.

The Duty of Offerings

Making Offerings to the Divine is of paramount importance because offering is the key to propitiating divine grace. Divine grace is a divine act that will assist you in growing spiritually. There are three main forms of Neterian offering. One is the Maat offering. The Maat offering is the offering of a Maat icon to the Divine (God or Goddess receiving the offering). There is more to making this offering than just the ritual; it means becoming virtuous, balanced, just and pure. The second offering is the arit. The arit is the "eye of Heru" in the form of consecrated food items, including bread, wine, beer, cakes etc. This offering represents the essence of Asar, and Heru that makes consciousness whole again. This offering was in place in the earliest period of recorded history in Ancient Egypt. The third form of offering is the "Hetep" Offering. This offering is an offering of duality. It is a tantric teaching that relates to offering one's individuality, merging oneself with the Divine and thereby dissolving the separation between individual consciousness and the Divine Self.

The final aspect of the Devotional practice to be considered, Meditation, will be discussed in its own chapter which immediately follows this one.

Conclusion

Needless to say, prior to my study of the teachings of Shetaut Neter, my idea of Devotion was nothing like this. Devotion in my practical world sense was centered on being devoted to my family. As a young person devotion was given to my parents and siblings. As a married adult, I was devoted to my wife and children.

"An Aspirant's Guide To Practicing The Egyptian Mysteries"

In the context of spirituality, Devotion was centered on the attempt to "save" others from the perils of a life of sin. I also saw Devotion as the regular attendance at religious gathering places. At its highest, Devotion to me at this earlier time in life was believing in a God that I had to both love and be afraid of. This God was also seen as an entity that was somewhere far off who I needed to save me from the sins I was born with.

Presently, as a student of the teachings of Shetaut Neter, my view of Devotion has now evolved beyond these earlier ideas. Although devotion can be practiced through the methods given above and even those given in other religious traditions, ultimately Devotion is a process designed to purify the emotional aspect of the personality. This is done by training you to see the Divine in everyone and everything. The mind of this person remains on the Divine at all times and never wavers effortlessly, similar to how the mind of a mother remains effortlessly on her child even as the mother involves herself in performing various duties.

Devotion to something entails love for that thing. What we choose to Love is the choice that must be made. The choice is twofold. Love the outer manifestation of someone or something or love the underlying essence which gives rise to and supports the outer manifestation of that someone or thing. Love for the Divine is infinite and eternal. Love for objects is temporary and illusory. As Love in its pure form is very strong and intense, learning the difference between loving in a worldly sense and loving God for me was/is a very big lesson that I am still learning. No matter how much I read in the teachings that the object of our love should be the Divine, I still have to focus on putting this into practice on a regular basis.

Upon further reflection, I now realize that the difficulty of keeping the Divine as the focus of our attention is because we are afraid to let go and love the Divine in a truly unconditional way which this is. Do you know how much love the Divine can give to us? That's a whole lot of juice! ☺ So fear of the unknown in this way hinders our ability to love in an unconditional way. Our ability is hindered because we unconsciously ask ourselves the following question. "How can I experience, let alone handle the Love from the Divine, when I haven't experienced real love in the world right now?"

Love for the Divine and the ability to experience it is the goal of the Devotional practices of Shetaut Neter. Purify your emotions so that you can experience real love. Love that is unconditional!

"An Aspirant's Guide To Practicing The Egyptian Mysteries"

Chapter 18

Meditation in Practice
Uaa

"Be still and solemn silence keep; then shall God open the way for salvation. Withdraw into thyself and Father-Mother God will come. Throw away the work of the body's senses and thy divinity will come to birth; purge from thyself the animal torments, concerns with things of matter."

"If thou wilt attentively dwell (meditate) and observe with thy heart's eyes, thou will find the path that leads above; nay that image shall become thy guide itself, because the divine sight hath this peculiar charm; it holdeth fast and draweth unto it those who succeed in opening their eyes, just as they say, the magnet and the iron."

-Ancient Egyptian Proverbs

No matter what level of the teachings you have reached, these two proverbs provide great insight into the practice of meditation. Reflection on them in time will bring intuitional realization of what is required to achieve spiritual liberation (salvation). Additionally, reflection on them provides knowledge of what interferes and hinders the spiritual movement.

If you have been raised in a western societal culture, your idea about what salvation is has been shaped by the belief that a certain "person" is necessary to "save" you from your sins. Even if you do not prescribe to this belief, the fact that the overwhelming majority of people believe this makes its impact on you a substantial one. This is another way that we can be conditioned. This is unfortunate because this way of thought about the nature of salvation and its means of attainment is a relatively new concept (2000 years old approximately). There is another thought much older that is being resurrected today.

The entire set of Neterian practices discussed thus far, when practiced in conjunction with meditation, allow a person the ability to experience an aspect of their nature that many have forgotten exists. This nature is what is being described in the proverbs above. Meditation is the final practice that when done correctly leads a person to the ancient ideas about what salvation is.

Again reflect deeply on these proverbs as you practice the Yogic disciplines until their insight is revealed to you. Until then recognize the following about meditation. Dr. Muata Ashby in his book, Meditation, The Ancient Egyptian Path To Enlightenment, says this about the meditative practice.

"Meditation may be thought of or defined as the practice of mental exercises and disciplines to enable you as the aspirant to achieve control over the mind due to unwanted thoughts and imaginations."

Essentially meditation is a practice that in time allows you to control your mind. As your mind is the repository of thoughts and desires, control of the mind means you are learning how to control what you think. In today's modern era this is a radical notion. Few believe that it is possible to control our mind. The prevailing thought today is that we have no control over what thoughts or ideas come into and go out of it. According to the teachings of Shetaut Neter and other ancient mystical traditions, this is the furthest thing from the truth.

Additionally, meditation is a discipline that will help you increase your awareness about yourself and the world around you. Awareness or consciousness can only be increased when your mind is in a state of peace and tranquility. Therefore control over your mind to eradicate agitation is enjoined for this purpose. The theory of meditation is that when the mind and senses are controlled and transcended, the awareness of the transcendental state of consciousness becomes clear. As this consciousness/awareness expands, you as the meditator will be able to discover forgotten abilities of the unconscious part of your mind.

When you are able to reach the heights of meditative experience a more continuous form of awareness will develop. It will not be lost at the time you fall asleep. This awareness will be present in the waking, dream, and dreamless sleeping states.

To reach these meditative heights, a meditative lifestyle should be developed along with your formal meditation practice. This means that you should begin acting in such a way that there is greater and greater detachment from objects and situations and greater independence and peace within. Therefore simultaneous with the formal meditation practice, a keen understanding of your deeper self and the nature of the world experience of human experience should be developed. This understanding can be fostered when the consumption of a vegetarian diet and exercise is included in your spiritual practices.

An aid in the development of this understanding is the recognition that people ordinarily do things to derive some pleasure or reward for doing them. You could say people do things for selfish reasons and you would be correct. Many acts are selfish because their unconscious and subconscious desires lead them to do things to satisfy those desires. Obtainment of pleasure and rewards are the reasons people do things. Unfortunately people don't realize that the pursuit of pleasures like this keeps their minds agitated.

Living a meditative way of life means that your actions are always affirmations of your higher knowledge and awareness and not based on the unconscious desires and emotions of your mind. Be aware that this takes practice and will not occur overnight. When this practice is perfected though, the rewards are many. One of the rewards will be the ability to clearly understand the meaning behind the proverbs presented at the beginning of this chapter. When you have a clear understanding of what they mean, smile and thank the Divine for the awareness that you now have.

"An Aspirant's Guide To Practicing The Egyptian Mysteries"

Smai Tawi

Chapter 19

The Three Fold Sheti Practice

It has been enjoined that an aspirant do his/her Sheti practice three times a day. The first in the morning as the sun rises usually between 4:00 am-6:00 am. The second should be done around the noon day hour. The final one should be done sometime between 6:00 pm-8:00 pm about the time of the setting of the Sun. When I began my initiatic practice I did my best to adhere to this schedule. I admit though that I did not fully understand the importance of the three fold practice at that time. In many ways it seemed to me like a ritual no different from what I had seen my Muslim friends do, who did their prayers five times a day. Although I was diligent with this practice at the beginning, I did not understand the significance of what was happening as I faithfully did my best to adhere to it.

I now understand that Nehast/Enlightenment will be very difficult to achieve in this lifetime if I am not doing the three- fold practice. As stated previously, the integrated practice of yoga thru the Sheti disciplines is a purification process. The process cleanses our physical, mental and spiritual bodies of things that are toxic to it. The physical body is cleansed of foods that make us more susceptible to being led by our emotions. Our mental bodies are cleansed of ideas which have us believe that the full extent of reality is that which we perceive thru our five senses. Toxins and chemicals are also cleansed which limit our ability to perceive reality as it actually is. Finally, the process allows the unconscious mental aspect of our being to be cleansed of "ari"/impressions which have us believe we are the body instead of spirit.

You will not fully know how firm a hold the world has on you until you begin your practice of the teachings. Its idea about life and how it is to be lived does not provide an environment for understanding the essential truth about existence. In fact, it has the exact opposite effect. It makes you a slave to an idea about life and how it is to be lived, based on an illusion. However, an illusion believed to be real over lifetimes feels like everything but an illusion. It "feels" real! Anything short of a three fold cleansing practice is really nothing more than an intermittent haphazard process. Although spiritually no action goes unnoticed and provides some type of benefit, Nehast is achieved by those who are one pointed in their pursuit of this goal. The aspirant who seeks perfection in living righteously while engaged in any activity while actually believing that perfection is possible is in a strong position to achieve Nehast in this lifetime. Therefore, the three fold Sheti

"An Aspirant's Guide To Practicing The Egyptian Mysteries"

practice is necessary because the depth of cleansing/purification necessary is much deeper than we can truly know at the beginning of our practice.

I liken the three- fold Sheti practice to putting on a coat of armor. In an earlier era, armor was worn to protect a person from blows in battles. A person without his armor had no protection from punishment that was coming on the battlefield. I now realize through personal experience, that experiencing life in the day to day world is very similar to a battlefield. There are all sorts of so-called sense distractions and pleasures. There are many people seeking to satisfy their sense pleasures. For these people, this is the purpose of life. These people may outwardly encourage you to "live" a little because "you only live once." Even for those aspirants who do not have friends tempting them like this, seeing life lived in this way by almost everyone creates a "magnetic type of force" which can impel a person to act as others do. Combine this with our personal "ari"/unconscious impressions and you have a force that will be difficult to withstand. This makes the world appear to be very alluring. This "magnetic" quality and "ari" attracts people to the appearance of the world and the objects within it. This magnetic attraction combined with a belief that sense pleasures must be pursued and satisfied makes moving beyond this mindset a "difficult" task to say the least.

I now liken the three fold daily practice to being inside the temple walls in Ancient Kamit, sheltered from the world, to learn the teachings until a certain period of time when you come out to practice what you have learned in that setting. Since we do not have temples today, the area in our home reserved for our daily practice becomes our temple and the attendance at Conferences and other spiritually uplifting events constitute our pilgrimages.

Most people react to every emotional whim or desire that they have. However, in our practice, we are learning how to create a distance between our ego which houses these emotional whims and desires and our Higher Self which we have forgotten exists. The three- fold Sheti practices create a bridge that makes it easier to first see the separation and then stay on the opposite side of our ego.

Without the three fold practice, the pressure to react to your senses will overpower you since this is all you have known in this and previous lifetimes. Therefore this practice is necessary until we become established in our Higher Self which moves the ego into its service and is no longer influenced by it. When this happens, your daily worship schedule will turn into a moment by moment worship of the Divine. You will then see the underlying essence that gives rise to, is behind, and sustains creation every second. After practicing the three fold worship for years, it will become a habit so even after Nehast is realized, you may continue practicing out of habit and to inspire and train aspirants.

Without the concerted effort to practice in this way at the beginning, your movement can quickly become disjointed. For example, you may be very disciplined with your morning Sheti practice. This creates the armor spoken of previously which creates distance between your Higher Self and ego/lower self. Sometimes you will be able to feel yourself as a "witness" to your thoughts and emotional states. Others may tell you that it seems like you are "glowing" or that you have an "air" about you. This should not be surprising and is common. Unfortunately this "glow" and the other after effects from the morning practice will only armor you for so long. In three to five hours, the charge will diminish and you will need to recharge your batteries. In short you will need a boost. This is when it is time for the afternoon Sheti practice.

As a new aspirant you will likely be diligent with the three- fold practice for the first two - four years. However, as time goes on and your circumstances change (new or different job or new relationship etc.), your ability to be stationary during the afternoon and evening hours may not be possible. For many the morning Sheti will not stop but the other two may become a hit and miss proposition. If this occurs, be mindful that this new disjointed practice will also make your ability to handle the world become disjointed also. The ego/Set fights so hard that you don't always realize that your conduct in the world is not in accordance with Maat.

For example you may find yourself at times eating pizza and drinking soda and justifying it. You may pursue companionship for the purpose of sense pleasures and justify it by saying that you just want to be friends. Subtly and maybe without awareness, your ability to handle life issues in a balanced and orderly way gives way to emotion and pride. All of this can happen while engaged in a steady morning Sheti practice only. I know this can happen because this is a common occurrence for those on the path.

It is best to put yourself in a position to master yourself as quickly as possible. This means that it is best for all concerned that you give yourself the best opportunity grow in the teachings everyday. Be mindful that as students of the teachings, we are not immune from the challenges of the world. It still takes seconds or minutes to get into a situation and months or years to get out of one. The goal is to practice the teachings in a way in which you don't create any new negative drama/ari for yourself. In this way all you will have to deal with is the negative "ari" that you created previously. This is a good thing as there is an end to this road. Until Nehast dawns, you will still be accumulating ari so what you want to do is accumulate positive ari and impressions which are lucid. Negative dull and agitated ari creates entanglements. As soon as you have dealt with all of your past "ari" you're done. No more drama. No more strife. No more worry. A life of joy, peace and contentment awaits the person able to stop creating drama in the present moment.

However not creating negative "ari" is much easier said than done. This creation occurs far more frequently during those parts of the day when we miss our afternoon or evening Sheti practice. Without our armor, it is easy to fall prey to our innermost desires which have yet to be purified. This is why the three- fold practice is so important.

Although the three- fold daily Sheti practice will not eliminate all creation of new "ari," it helps in a substantial way. This is important because one of the purposes is to create a mind that is peaceful and contented. Developing a mind like this is much easier when we stop creating unnecessary drama in our lives. Resultantly, Nehast will be achieved faster when we create the environment best suited for its attainment. This is done when we engage in the three- fold Sheti practice.

Chapter 20

Conclusion

THE SCALES OF MAAT AND THE PSYCHOSPIRITUAL ENERGY CENTERS

I recently heard Dr. Muata Ashby (Sebai Maa) say that "the method provided to us for achieving Nehast from the Sages of Ancient Kemet should be practiced like it's a science." I am paraphrasing what I heard him say, but the meaning behind it will become clear shortly.

After much reflection and thought on this I have come to realize the profound wisdom behind this statement. When an endeavor is approached from a scientific perspective, all aspects of it are placed in the optimal position to receive the optimal result. When a scientific experiment is done, everything needed for it is gathered together and cleansed and placed in an environment that will produce the best result. The best result is a result free from bias or error. If a particular location is to be used for the experiment, the location is cleansed and sanitized. This might mean extra cleaning of the floors, walls and other areas as debris could disrupt both the performance and experiment's findings.

What should be noted is that when conducting a science experiment, attention to every detail is done to ensure that the data obtained is reliable. The integrated practice of the teachings of Shetaut Neter was designed to be practiced like it is a scientific experiment. The teachings affirmatively make clear that anyone who is an authentic aspirant, who practices an authentic teaching under the guidance of an authentic teacher, will derive Nehast. The teachings are very clear on this. The way we practice the teachings and our mindset about its practice will either quicken or slow our spiritual development, growth and evolution.

The everyday practice of the teachings in our everyday lives is nothing short of conducting a scientific experiment. We cleanse and purify the location where we will be conducting the experiment, our body, mind and soul, and then do the actual experiment itself which for us is the integrated practice of Shetaut Neter. In due time and due season, the Divine bestows "conscious realization" or "awakening" of the underlying essence behind all of Creation on the practitioner. At this point you can say that the scientific experiment was a resounding success.

However, failure to prepare the area where the scientific experiment is going to take place will skew the experiments results. One way this happens on the path is that many of us approach the practice of Shetaut Neter like any other religious practice. This is very easy to do given the fact that most of the people we interact with (family, friends, co-workers etc) talk religion but don't live it. Few practice what they preach. This environmental so-called norm leaves us with an impression of what the practice of religion looks like. Although we may look at disdain at other religious practices that differ from ours, the inescapable fact is that on an unconscious level, we have grown accustomed to a "talk about religious" practice as opposed to a "live it practice" of religion.

This "talk about religion" impression interferes and slows down a person's ability to properly cleanse the area where the scientific experiment is going to take place which is the body, mind and soul.

Care must be given to not falling into the trap of treating the practice of Shetaut Neter like it is any other religious practice. This is difficult given the fact that most in western society have grown up hearing that "all are born sinners." The underlying message in this type of thinking is that a person does not have the capacity to achieve perfection or a perfected state. This provides an easy out and gives no incentive to live life in a way that a perfected state is realized. This allows people to fall prey to every whim and emotional state because since a person cannot control himself or herself anyway. This makes practicing religion in this way; "easy" because all you have to do is just "talk the talk" and not "walk the walk!" With this mindset a person does not ever have to take full responsibility for every aspect of their personality.

But when the integrated practice of Shetaut Neter is treated like a science, that mentality is immediately changed. This type of aspirant is serious about the experimental process. This aspirant is always on the lookout for performing each step in the process as well as possible. If the teachings say spiritualize every thing done in the world, they constantly look to do that. When feeling emotional stimulation of love for their mate, they recognize that this part of the experiment requires them to look at this "feeling" as actually being a "feeling" for the Divine. When performing actions in the world, they recognize that this part of the experiment requires them to "see" that it is the Divine actually performing the actions and not them.

A mindset that treats the integrated practice of Shetaut Neter as a science makes it much easier to spiritualize every thing done in the course of a day. This is what it means to actually practice religion. This is what it means to live it, reaching the point where every thought and every action of the person automatically flows to the Divine. This is what the scientific approach will do for the aspirant. When every moment is spiritualized, Nehast is assured!

With that said, consider the following:

What If It's True?

Many people have heard the phrase "we are spiritual beings having a human experience!" I now ask you the reader, what if this is true? Right now in this very moment, what if the reality is that we are actually spiritual beings having an intermittent human experience? Would that change your outlook on life? Would it change how you feel about a variety of things?

This differs greatly from the opposite common belief that we are human beings having intermittent spiritual experiences. The spirit is more akin to energy which is very subtle. If spirit is in fact the core of who we are shouldn't that change the current view of what we consider life to be and how it is to be lived?

Below for your consideration is a list of questions that I ask you in the context of the question "what if it's true that we are spiritual beings having a human experience." Answer each question yes or no.

1. If it is true that a person is actually Spirit, not flesh, should your idea about what death is change? (If I am Spirit I am eternal therefore there is no such thing as death as it is known presently.)

2. If it is true that a person is actually Spirit, not flesh, should your idea about what life is and how it is to be lived change? (If I am actually Spirit, then life as I have known it is more akin to an isolated intermittent experience rather than anything abiding. Therefore is there a need to "ever" get upset, mad, frustrated, discontent, jealous, envious or others? Aren't these emotional states borne from the belief that our abiding reality is flesh of the body?)

3. If it is true that a person is actually Spirit not flesh, should your idea about what happiness is change? (Present ideas about happiness are built around the obtainment of objects and satisfaction of sense pleasures. These satisfactions are limited and keep a person in a constant chase for more limited satisfaction experiences. Anything limited is not real. Since these experiences are not real, can this idea about what happiness is be real either?)

4. If it is true that a person is actually Spirit not flesh, should your ideas about what love is change? (Present ideas about what love is centers around the feeling I get from emotional impulses and stimulation received as a result from interaction with another person. Unless emotions are directly tied into the spiritual aspect of my being, can this truly be what actual love is?)

5. If it is true that a person is actually Spirit not flesh, should your ideas about what emotions are change? (Emotions are the by-product of value determinations that a person makes about a variety of things. For instance when I place a value on something by saying "I like this," then emotional states of like or even love develop based upon that value judgment. An opposite emotion is also created when this happens automatically although it happens unconsciously. Dislike for the opposite state is immediately created. How can a value determination made from the perspective that a person is human be true if we are in fact Spirit?)

6. If it is true that a person is actually Spirit not flesh, should your ideas about what religion is and what its purpose is change? (Wouldn't a religious practice then be seen as a means towards completely "awakening" to and realizing that this spiritual essence is the sum total of who we are?)

7. If it is true that a person is actually Spirit not flesh, should your ideas about their relationship to people, animals, and nature change? (If I am in fact a manifestation of spirit, wouldn't this also mean that everything else is a manifestation of Spirit also? Wouldn't ideas of individuality and separateness have to give way to the reality of oneness and inclusion?)

8. If it is true that a person is actually Spirit not flesh, should their ideas about what a "soul mate" is change? (If my soul is actually one with all that exists right now in this moment, how could it ever mate with itself?)

Family, do not ever forget this fact. IT IS TRUE! We are Spiritual Beings having an intermittent human experience. The scientific experiment is now complete and I can proudly say that it has been a resounding success!

PEACE AND BLESSINGS!

"An Aspirant's Guide To Practicing The Egyptian Mysteries"

PRODUCTS BY THE AUTHOR

BOOKS

"YOU!

ARE RESPONSIBLE FOR YOUR LIFE!

"*You*, Are Responsible For Your Life!" is a modern day book of philosophy for the 21st century that provides "practical" advice to assist the reader in living life more spiritually. The person who wants to know the answer to the question, "Who Am I." It is a must read for those people of today who believe that "we are spiritual beings having a human experience." It is also a must read for the person who wants to take Complete control over every aspect of their personality.

Ultimately the book is about our ***IDEAS.*** What they are. What they are not. How they

"An Aspirant's Guide To Practicing The Egyptian Mysteries"

color and influence our perception of reality. An influence which often keeps us stuck in decades old behavior patterns that prevent us from having the type of life we want. A life of perpetual joy, peace and happiness.

ISBN: 0978634608
Cost: $15.99

"A BLACK MAN, MY POINT OF VIEW"

OVERCOME MALE/FEMALE RELATIONSHIP DRAMA IN THE AFRICAN-AMERICAN COMMUNITY.

"A Black Man, My Point of View," was written to help couples achieve what many say they want. A relationship that fulfills their dreams and desires. Unfortunately, very few people ever achieve this state in their relationship. In fact it is more common than not that a person can live their entire life and never achieve one relationship like this. Even couples married for 25+ years in many cases are unhappily married. What is happening in our community that does not allow couples to achieve the state that many yearn for?

People do not realize that the foundation of relationship drama is formed at the beginning when relationships start. In fact, I assert that the demise of a relationship is certain based upon that foundation. It is not a matter of if. It is a matter of when. Relationship drama

"An Aspirant's Guide To Practicing The Egyptian Mysteries"

unfolds as unconscious behavior patterns direct and impel a person to act in ways that negatively impact the relationship. These patterns are known as "drivers" and are revealed. Solutions are provided to overcome them.

ISBN: 0978634616
Cost: $13.99

A NOTE ABOUT THE AUTHOR

LAWRENCE R. MATHEWS (ANPU WASET) WAS BORN AND RAISED IN DETROIT, MICHIGAN. HE IS THE FIRST IN HIS IMMEDIATE FAMILY TO GRADUATE FROM COLLEGE, COMPLETING HIS STUDIES AT WESTERN MICHIGAN UNIVERSITY IN 1986 WHERE HE RECEIVED A BACHELOR OF BUSINESS ADMINISTRATION, B.B.A. DEGREE. HE IS ALSO THE FIRST TO ATTEND GRADUATE SCHOOL, COMPLETING HIS STUDIES AT MICHIGAN STATE UNIVERSITY DETROIT COLLEGE OF LAW IN 1996 WHERE HE RECEIVED A JURIS DOCTOR, J.D. DEGREE.

MR. MATHEWS WORKED AS AN EDUCATOR FOR THE DETROIT PUBLIC SCHOOLS FOR APPROXIMATELY EIGHT YEARS AND AS AN ATTORNEY FOR NINE YEARS. HE HAS PRACTICED BEFORE THE MICHIGAN SUPREME COURT, THE MICHIGAN COURT OF APPEALS, AND HAS HAD MORE THAN 25 JURY TRIALS MAINLY AS A CIVIL DEFENSE ATTORNEY.

MR. MATHEWS IS THE FATHER OF TWO DAUGHTERS KHADEEJA AND NAILAH, AND IS THE GRANDFATHER OF ELIJAH.

ANPU WASET IS THE AFRICAN KEMETIC NAME CHOSEN BY MR. MATHEWS. IT MEANS "OPENER OF THE WAY" AND "GUIDE TO ENLIGHTENMENT."

MR. MATHEWS IS THE CREATOR OF THE **"INSPIRATIONAL PHILOSOPHY"** LECTURE SERIES. "INSPIRATIONAL PHILOSOPHY" IS THE STUDY AND APPLICATION OF ANCIENT KAMITIC PHILOSOPHICAL SYSTEMS WHICH ARE APPLIED TO COMMON SITUATIONS OF TODAY IN AN INSPIRATIONAL WAY. HIS OTHER INTERESTS INCLUDE THE PRACTICE OF YOGA, MEDITATION, AND VEGETARIANISM. HE STUDIES ANCIENT PHILOSOPHIES AND RELIGIONS. HE IS CURRENTLY A PRACTITIONER OF EGYPTIAN YOGA AND A STUDENT AND PRACTICING YOGI AT THE SEMA INSTITUTE AND UNIVERSITY OF YOGA IN MIAMI, FLORIDA.

"An Aspirant's Guide To Practicing The Egyptian Mysteries"

www.ingramcontent.com/pod-product-compliance
Lightning Source LLC
Chambersburg PA
CBHW060531100426
42743CB00009B/1490